THE DEVIL OF AMERICA
WANTS ME!
MY MEMOIR

CHIOMA AFOKE

authorHOUSE®

AuthorHouse™
1663 Liberty Drive
Bloomington, IN 47403
www.authorhouse.com
Phone: 833-262-8899

Published by AuthorHouse 01/12/2021

ISBN: 978-1-6655-1280-0 (sc)
ISBN: 978-1-6655-1278-7 (hc)
ISBN: 978-1-6655-1279-4 (e)

Library of Congress Control Number: 2021900257

CHAPTER ONE

The Devil of America wants me!

I WAS BORN DIFFERENTLY, I WAS fashioned a certain way, with unique features and character.

I stayed in my mother's womb almost one year. Normal babies stay in the womb for nine months on the average, but I guess I was not normal from the womb. After eleven months, I was forced out of my mother's womb. When I came out, I was so sick and jaundiced. Recovered from it, and on my way home from the hospital, I was arrested.

Arrested by the police

Mama and I was on our way home from the hospital, being driven by daddy's friend whom he sent to get us because he had to be at work. My father being a civil service employee had to work that day. He sent his friend to pick his wife up from the hospital, after the delivery of their tenth child. Yes, I am my parents' tenth child.

My parent had many boys and my mother insisted on getting a second daughter. She had her first girl after her six boys, and in the process of trying for her a second daughter, she had three more boys before I came.

While returning home from the hospital, police at the check point discovered that the driver had some missing documents for his car, they decided to arrest the driver.

You see, in Nigeria, arrests are made differently. As a driver of a vehicle, once you are arrested for any traffic offense, you are taken to the police station including your car and everything in the car. This particular day, when the arrest was made, my mother and the newborn had to go as well. While we were there at the police station, my big brother came into the station, and I was told he beat up the policeman who arrested us, nothing became of that case, because the Divisional Police Officer (DPO) who is the top-ranking police officer in the area; on being alerted about the incident, dismissed the case and faulted the police officer for arresting a driver carrying a newborn.

Growing up

I remember being around my mother a lot, since I was her last baby. My mother took me to many of the church meetings she attended. God picked on me from the womb, he knew the battles ahead and he programmed me from the womb. Yes, I was chosen and sent forth from the womb.

I just remember that I treated myself differently, I didn't do many things that other kids did. My mother had me monitored closely. She restricted my movements most times. She would not allow me to do many things that other kids did. I was not allowed to go moon chasing like other kids, lots of bad things happened during moon chasing, wayward children mingling with others and crazy things happening to them.

My mother from the beginning banned moon chasing. No body dared my mother. I watched her discipline my brothers, and I realized I wouldn't want her to ever discipline me that way. She was like a tigress; just obey her instructions and you were fine.

I had many restrictions growing up and as a result of that, I had to follow her to numerous places. I wasn't allowed to play outside with other kids when it was dark. Those were the best times to play, because kids from other neighboring communities would come around, and we would play different games. I thought she was too protective, and that's why I wasn't allowed to do some of the things other kids did. Now, I truly appreciate the fact that my mother was prepared by God to protect what she was given, a unique child.

Sacred Heart Catholic Church

This was the church we attended. My parents still do. Even at a very tender age, while attending benedictions on Sunday evenings, strange things would happen to me. Things I couldn't explain and had no gut to ask anyone. My thoughts was that I wasn't normal, and I wasn't going to tell anyone the things that were happening to me, because I wasn't sure what they would think of me.

During benedictions, when the priest would lift up the blessed sacrament, my hands would tingle with some warmth feelings rushing through my fingers and palms. These sensations grew stronger and stronger, and made me really uncomfortable.

The only thing was that, after the services, I would feel elevated in my heart, with a level of peace. Something was happening to me, but I had no one to explain to me what it was. At a point, I thought I had the devil who was trying to jump out of my body through my hands, and it made me even more uncomfortable, because I wouldn't want anyone to notice what I was experiencing.

Then one Sunday, during morning mass, I was in the children's church during an Easter Sunday; the priest raised the chalice, during communion benediction and my eyes opened to an image on it. The face of Jesus Christ as he was crucified on the cross. I closed my eyes, and opened it again, and he was still there. This time, I continued to look at the chalice until this face disappeared. I was just nine years old when this happened to me, and I remember the face very well because we had just finished the lent season. Still, I couldn't speak to anyone about it, because I wasn't sure what they would think of me? I didn't know if I would be told that I had the devil in me. That used to scare me, because I remembered those who were told that they had the devil, would go through some process of deliverance, which also included going without food for some days, and attending retreats. I never liked anything about the devil, and still don't.

CHAPTER TWO

Religious practices

MOTHER TOOK ME EVERYWHERE AND mostly church going. I grew up watching my mother leave very early in the morning for morning masses. My mother was very religious and at a very tender age, she taught us religion. She would wake us up as early as five in the morning to pray the rosary. Yes, it was our routine. Everyone in my house participated in early morning prayer which was mostly counting the rosary. Sometimes five decades, meaning just one rosary, but at nights we prayed fifteen decades, which was like counting the beads round three times, especially if we are making any special request to God through Mary.

The VOW

When I turned nine years, I and my mother visited a popular Holy Ghost Reverend Father, called Father Emmanuel Edeh. He is a Nigerian Roman Catholic priest of the Holy Ghost congregation.

He is the founder of a pilgrimage center called Eucharistic Adoration Center, in Elele, Rivers State of Nigeria. This Holy Ghost center is popularly known as Elele.

In those days, Elele was known to be the final terminal for any form of spiritual problems. That's where almost everyone who had issues with evil attacks, sicknesses, infirmities, and any form of family or communal disputes went to seek, and to get help.

Elele was also known as a place where you go to meet with God, a place of encounters. Whenever you encounter God, there must be a change in your life. The part of the change people experienced in Elele was in the form of healing, family restorations and the end of evil attacks etc.

Elele has now progressed to become more like a religious congregation center with medical facilities, homes for the orphans, the sick, the disabled, and the mentally ill. They also run soup kitchens, schools, counseling and conflict resolution programs.

When I visited Elele with my mother, we went there for a spiritual encounter, because my mother was believing God for something I didn't really know. I never really bothered to find out. I was engrossed with the encounters and my experiences; Elele was a spiritually charged atmosphere. How did I know this? because it felt different in that environment. It felt like God was closer, and it was a feeling one couldn't really explain.

On one of those visits, I remember very well the reverend Father at Elele (Father Edeh) as he is popularly called, announcing for those who wanted to dedicate their lives to the service of God to come to the altar and make a vow to God for His service.

I told my mother that I would like to go forward; there was a big force inside of me that made me uncomfortable and was pulling me to that vow. When I told my mother, she told me to make sure that I knew what I was doing. She asked me questions before she allowed me to move forward. Nonetheless, when I got to the front of the altar, Father Elele told me that I was not making any mistakes and that God led me to the altar. Additionally, he blessed me with the others that came forward to make that vow.

Now, coming back home from Elele, my mother reminded me about the vow, and told me how important it relates to living a consecrated life, and she said I cannot live my life the way others lived. Although I didn't really understand what it entails to live a consecrated live, I just resolved to be a good girl, meaning no telling lies, no stealing anyone's food; those were the major offenses in our house.

You were not allowed to lie to my mother, and you were not allowed to steal food from your siblings' plates. The level of atrocities that are seen today were not common in my community, or better off, I was not exposed to such.

That's what growing up was like with my mother. She took me along to the many places she visited. My mum belonged to many religious societies within the Catholic Church, and I equally belonged to them too. Some of the societies included the guild of St Anthony and Legion of Mary. I was very active in these organizations even at a very young age. By the time I was a preteen, I was already leading the junior leagues.

The Marian Village

My elder brother Christopher was in his senior seminary, on his way to becoming a Roman Catholic priest. Suddenly, he decided he was leaving the seminary to a place dedicated to the service of the Blessed Virgin Mary, the mother of Jesus. He announced his decision to my parents, that he was called to a deeper service where he would not interact much with the world.

My parents were divided on that matter, but my mother was in support of him to pursue a higher calling, which was what he called it.

When it was time, my brother Christopher left for the Marian village located in Adada within Nsukka of Enugu State Nigeria. Brother Christopher was there for about three months and returned to take all of our family to the Marian village. According to my brother, the man of God over that community received a mandate from heaven for everyone to go back and rescue all their families. The Marian village was supposedly the new Noah's ark. He said what was coming ahead was going to befall people who were not in this community (the ark), just like the days of Noah.

We were so ignorant; we didn't read the Bible for ourselves as Catholics. We lived by what we were told by the priests. Furthermore, catholic priests are so much revered and that's why so many congregants fall victim to ignorance.

Nonetheless, when my brother gave this news to my parents, daddy said no one was going anywhere. One of my elder brother's Godwin decided he would join brother Christopher in the pursuit of this higher calling. And they insisted my mother let them take me with them to help protect my future; I was the only angelic tender and innocent one around. My mother was able to convince my father to let me go with them. My bag was packed, and I left with my two brothers to the Marian village.

In this village (a gated community), you were assigned a room according to your age and gender. Males stayed in one side of the building, while the females stayed in another side of the building.

One common ground was the cafeteria and the worship center.

We had routines, starting with the early morning mass at 5:30AM. However, before the morning mass, you were expected to wake up from your bunk bed by 4:30AM, to wash up, brush your teeth and get dressed. Everyone was expected to be in the sanctuary before the holy mass. I never thought of what would have happened if you didn't wake up to follow the routine. We just obeyed the rules.

Something was weird about this place. We lived like the monks; although the teenage girls once they turned eighteen years, were allowed to get married. They were allowed to get married, but not to any other man in this community. Marriage was only permitted to a man called Servus Maria, who was exalted as a man of God and he was the head of the community. Servus Maria lived in the underground section of the male building and had a different cook from the general cook, who made his meals. The personal service and the general upkeep of Servus Maria was applied differently from the rest of the community. Additionally, there was a section of the cafeteria, that was secluded from the general space, where no one was allowed to go into, except those who were attached to Servus Maria. Furthermore, those who went into that section with him were mostly a particular set of sisters and brothers.

Nevertheless, when the young girls become sixteen years, they move into a different wing allocated specifically for them, in order to start training to become married. They attended classes and went through ceremonial preparations. Once a girl was deemed ready, a marriage ceremony was performed in the sanctuary.

The marriage ceremony was not like the usual marriage ceremony.

Here the books of Songs of Solomon was recited by the young girl. The preparation involved learning to recite all the chapters of the songs of Solomon by heart.

While she recited the songs of Solomon, the one who stood in as her husband was the founder of the place, the man referred to as the man of God by name Servus Maria. He would respond to the songs being recited as if he was king Solomon; the Beloved. In other words, the teenage girl was the fairest among them all, to this man who is in turn her king Solomon.

After the ceremony in the sanctuary, she is worn a ring by this king, and it's followed by a ceremonial celebration in the cafeteria.

It's usually a big ceremony where people dressed up like they were attending an actual wedding. During the after-wedding celebration, cakes were presented to them and they cut the cake. Then followed by a ceremonial dance. This is the one time I actually enjoyed this community. In the course of six months that I lasted there, I witnessed about three weddings. Yes, three different girls were married to this one man.

Oh, need I forget! After the wedding, the young girl would move into the part of the underground house where the man lived. They were allowed to spend time with him for one week or more.

After which they are joined back into the women's building.

How did I know these things? I was just an eleven-year-old girl. It's been an amazing characteristic that God blessed me with. I am very observant, and I can easily interpret behaviors that I observe. Sometimes, I tend to be in denial especially if the behavior is coming from someone, I think I know really well.

The Rescue mission: Justice Patrick Uhuo

Patrick Uhuo, who later became a Judge, is one of my big brothers who didn't believe in the story surrounding the Marian Village.

On this fateful day, after lunch, I was told that we had a visitor in the community and the visitor was my big brother who was a lawyer. My brother who visited home from Jos where he was staying at that time was informed by my mother that I was taken to the Marian village by my brothers. My brother was enraged, and the following morning he was on his way to the Marian village.

When I saw him in the visitor's lounge within the gated community, I was happy. Yes, there was a visitor's lounge immediately after the gate.

Meaning, once you get in, it's hard to get out. The lounge was located after the gate, far from the buildings. But anyone could easily sight the visitor from upstairs where the cafeteria was located. That's where I sighted him from, and I was really excited to see him. Initially, I thought he was coming to check the place out in case he wants to join us. I wasn't allowed to go to the visitor's lounge unless I was called upon. I was waiting to be called upon to see my brother; but was given a surprising news. The head of the girl's room, called me aside, and told me I might be going home. I didn't know one had a chance to go home once they were received into the village. But my case was different, he threatened to sue them for abduction. He told them that I was very tender to be housed in a community setting like that. He said, I would have to come home with him, and once I turned eighteen which is the legal age, I could return to the community if I wanted.

The big guys which included the Servus Maria, the Priest and other notable leaders were all in the visitor's lounge where I could hear my brother yelling at my other two brothers for bringing me to the community.

Finally, the matter was concluded, I was called upon to see my brother. I went into the visitor's lounge crying because I wasn't sure if I wanted to really go home. I was a little afraid of what the Marian community said was going to befall the whole world.

My big brother, Patty Uhuo was in his usual element. He quickly yelled at me to keep quiet and go get my stuff so he can take me home. Not sure what to do, I stood there staring at him, the girl's leader who escorted me to the lounge told me stop crying. She told me that Servus Maria had already agreed that my brother was right to come for me, because my parents were not in the community with me to decide my fate. She said I should come with her so I can pack up my bag, and pacified me that once I turned eighteen, they would come to take me back if I wanted. I packed my little bag and followed my brother. Once we were outside the gate, toward the street, I was so relieved. It felt differently to be back in the world of normal people.

Once we got home, my friends gathered round me to hear my story, they wanted to know what happened to me. I was as bald as a bald eagle.

Once you got into the community, you are shaved bald, and given a head cover. No one was allowed to have hairs upon their head. That's why when I returned home with my brother, I was bald. I sat a certain way with both hands together like one who was praying. The only time you weren't holding both hands together was when you were eating or in the bathroom.

At home, that evening, I still folded my hands as if I was in the Marian village. My friends were amazed at my current attitude and behavior. Nevertheless, those behavior disappeared after one week and I became almost my normal self. Although I was more religious than usual. I still practiced my prayer routines just like we did in the community. In the Marian Village, we prayed the rosary four times in a day and sang songs of psalms and hymns.

I had just finished my Elementary school before my trip to the Marian village and on getting back, the results for common entrance examination were just released.

My elder brother Patty Uhuo made sure I was registered to start my Junior high school (JSS1) before he went back to Jos.

After few weeks of adjustment, I was packaged and well prepared for my junior high school, which was a boarding school.

CHAPTER THREE

A twist, the beginning of the plan

Junior High School (Ezza Girls Secondary School)

S CHOOL WAS FUN, ESPECIALLY THE fact that I was away from home and most of my childhood friends attended the same school. The school was the only "ALL" girls' high school in my city.

In loving school, I also was excellent at learning and very skilled in school activities. We had a school choir, and I was the leader of the church choir by JSS2, and not only this, we had competitions with other community schools within the vicinity which was really engaging.

Nonetheless, by Junior Secondary School Class 3, we were known for greatness in my school, but I had to quiet down a bit from school activities due to my preparation for the Junior High School exam called the Junior WEAC.

My Sister

My sister got married when I was in my JSS3. Her traditional marriage was the talk of the town. You have to understand that I lived in a small city, very local but a fun place. I couldn't have wished to grow up in a better city than Onueke. It was a city where everyone knew everyone's family and relatives. My family was popular because of the kind of brothers that

I have. A family of thirteen (including mom and dad) and I have nine big brothers. I have nine big brothers, gracious God they are all alive today.

When my sister got married, almost everyone who knew my family was in attendance. There were plenty of food and drinks. She married a rich husband according to the standard in those days. A man who was at that time a bank manager in the Central Bank of Nigeria. My parents were proud to be giving their first daughter away to a man who was well known to be financially compliant, because they believed she would be taken care of very well.

Nevertheless, by September of the following year, my sister was in need for help. She had a baby who just turned one year, and she was expecting her second baby. I had already spent some of my holiday helping her out while I was waiting for my Junior WEAC results.

My mother came to Enugu where she lived with her husband and brought the exciting news of the arrival of the Junior WEAC results which I performed phenomenally well. My daddy had asked her to come get me so I could prepare for Senior High School.

Few weeks after I left my sister's house, my father visited her and was told by my sister that she discussed with her husband and because of my brilliant results from the Junior WEAC, they decided to get me into a school in Enugu in order to help me better my education. My daddy was happy, and because my sister had told him that it was very urgent, she insisted that I return to Enugu immediately, so that I can start the registration process, since school had been two weeks into the new term.

My father being excited for me, came straight to my school where I had already settled in for the fresh senior high school. I was already rolling in my new experience as a senior in school. Being a senior meant a lot, because that's when you start preparing for school ranks. Senor Secondary Class 2, is when you become the real hard nut to crack. You pick other junior students who would serve you, help in fetching water and run other little errands. I was already looking forward to it, when suddenly my daddy appeared in my school. That was very weird, because my daddy hardly had time to visit me in school, due to the nature of his job. My mother worked as a cook in my school, so I get to see her every week.

When daddy showed up, he asked to speak to my principal, and while in the principal's office, I was called in, he broke the news to me.

My principal then Mrs. Margret Nwali was very excited for me, but she lamented that I was one of her brilliant students, and she was going to miss me.

My daddy waited for me in the visitor's lounge while I went to my hostel to pack up my things. I had no chance to say goodbye to my friends. I just told them I was going to Queen's school in Enugu.

Queen's School was a popular school in Enugu; every bright girl would have been excited to be in Queens' school and my classmates were very excited for me. Anyway, we got home, and the following morning, daddy took me to Enugu. He dropped me off at my sister's house and left that same day.

The Beginning of My Nightmare

Due to the urgency in my father's voice and how he whisked me away from my school, I thought that by the next day I would be in my new school at Enugu. That wasn't the case, rather I spent that week at my sister's house running errands for her.

I started cooking, cleaning, and taking care of my little Nephew who just turned one. I was happy taking care of my nephew because I had always longed to take care of little ones, since I was the last born in my family.

After the second week, making it the final week of the first month of school, I started getting uncomfortable and I asked my sister what was going on. I was met with the shock of my life. My sister told me that the school principal of the Holy Rosary College (HRC), an all-girls catholic school which is by far better than the Queen's college, which was supposedly my earlier promoted destination for schooling, had suggested that since I had already missed the registration for that school term, it would be better for me to start schooling in the second term.

Furthermore, my sister devised another plan. She took me to an all Girls' high school about a mile from her house and registered me there. In her argument, it wouldn't be right for me to stay at home for the next two months without schooling. The HRC had a very strict registration deadline and I missed that.

However, I told my sister that I would rather go back to my old school, then return when the HRC would accept my registration.

That was when my nightmares began to unfold. At this point, I began to get angry, but my anger amounted to nothing, because she was a sister that I looked up to, and I didn't really want to put her on the edge. I wanted to please her, so I stayed with her, watching her baby and trying to adapt to the new school.

This new school, which was the Trans-Ekulu girl's secondary school, had no boarding house. The students commuted to school by any means which included trekking, and this was my imposed choice of going to school.

The arrangement was very disturbing to me because, I was already used to the boarding school and focusing on my academics. The new routine was particularly difficult. I needed to do some house chores before going to school in the morning, then more cleaning, washing of the kids' clothes when I returned home from school. Additionally, there was no washing machine, so I hand washed my nephew's dirty clothes every day and I wasn't used to that at all. I continued like this until the two months were gone and I was so happy. My excitement was based on the expectation that by the next term, I would be in a new school and living in the boarding house.

Before the six weeks holiday period was over, I reminded my sister every week to get me registered into the HRC before it's too late. She kept telling me she was on it, and that she was communicating with the principal.

Boom! School was open, and my sister gave me a very sad news. She said that the HRC school would cost a lot of money since it was a private school, and her husband said he couldn't pay that much money for me to go to the school. I was shattered. I cried my eyes out. And I told her I would like to go back to my old school because it's actually better than the roadside school I was attending. I told her that at least my daddy wasn't paying too much money for me to be in my previous school.

I loved school, and I loved the fact that I had distinctions in my results. Daddy was always happy whenever I brought my results home and offered me rewards for good grades.

By this time, my sister already had her second baby, a beautiful baby girl. The joy that sustained me at her house was watching my nephew and my niece. They were the most beautiful little babies I had ever seen. While I was so disappointed in what I was experiencing from my sister, and living an agonizing life, I was also comforted by the presence of my little ones, even though, it meant more work for me, but I didn't mind.

Now, let me tell you what really happened here. My sister talked my daddy into believing that she had already got a new school for me, and that the school wanted me to start soon, because the slot would be given to another student.

That's why my father left his busy schedule, came to my old school where I was already settled in for the first senior school term.

I was later made aware by my sister's husband's niece who was staying with them at that time that she had no plan of taking me to any school. What she had told them was that I was going to stay with her in order to help out since she was pregnant and had a one-year-old son at home. Her plan was for me to attend the school close to her house and come home to help her after school. Her husband's niece could not stay with her because she was also in the Senior high school and lived in the boarding house. Her closest choice was to lie to my father to get me out of school, because once the school was open, and everyone was gone, she was left all alone with her one-year-old.

I couldn't believe my own sister could do a thing like that, I was shocked to my bones, but I guess my journey of discovering who my sister was had just started.

My mother came to visit because of the new baby and stayed with us for three months. She watched everything that I was going through, but all she could do was to comfort me, persuading me to stay with her because she really needed my help. She wanted me to help my sister, since she was my only sister. What I didn't understand was why I had to do it; just to make her happy? That's how she was raised, to be happy as the only girl child for a while.

Failing Grades

I made all the sacrifices that I could, living with my sister, but I still enjoyed being around my nephew and my niece. When I got into Senior Secondary (SS) Class 2, which is usually the most important class in Senior High school. This is because you choose what course of study you were going to pursue in the university. Meaning based on your grades, you will be determined to either pursue science or Art degree.

By this time, my mom had already gone back, and my little nephew had to start school in other to give my sister a chance to spend time with the new baby.

It meant more work for me, I had to get him up in the morning for school, feed him and have him set for his daddy, my brother in law to drop him off at a nursery school one mile away from home. It was fun to watch him go to school in the morning.

One thing led to another, my sister's husband decided he wasn't going to be dropping him off at school in the morning any longer; it was taking time for him to do that, and he was getting to his office a little late.

Guess what? I started doing the school run. I would get him ready, then get ready for school too. His school was in an opposite direction to my school, which made it a little tough for me. I was given money for taxi. I would take a taxi with him in the morning to take him to school, then I walk back home from where I would walk to my own school. Some days, I got to school very late, after the school morning assembly.

Yet, I would also need to pick him up in the afternoon, because his school was only open until 12:00 o'clock in the afternoon.

My school lunch break was between11:30AM to 12:30pm. I would leave school during lunch break to get to his school on time. Once I picked him up, I would get a taxi to drop us off at the gate. I would get him into the house, get him changed into new clothes. Then my sister started requesting that I bathed him before changing him into new clothes. And some days she would request I feed him before returning back to school.

It was terrible, I wondered what was going to become of my life.

My academic was dying slowly, I was watching the things that I loved most being stolen from me, but I was helpless. I would get back to school late every day because of these issues. But I was helpless.

Physics was one of the classes that were offered in the afternoon immediately after break, so I would miss almost half of the class teaching.

By the end of the first term in SS2, I failed physics. I couldn't imagine going from a distinction in Mathematics, to failing physics. Like, I got an F as a grade in physics.

By the second term in SS2, I was disqualified from science as a major, because physics was one of the requirements to progressing into a science major.

I was so numb to what was happening to me, and it made me very quiet. People who saw me thought I was a quiet person, but if you knew me from my old school, I got in trouble for noise making. I was a happy kid in my family, until I started living with my sister.

More Shocks

Things started to pile up for me, by now my mother had come to check on me few more times, and she would comfort me, telling me to remember that people are watching to see what would become of my sister. I love and admire my mother very much, so I listened to whatever she had to say.

Due to the demand on me academically, I would stay up at night to finish my assignments and study for my quizzes. As a result, I wouldn't be able to make it to the 5:30AM rule my brother-in-law made that we had to wake up. I said we, because my mother on seeing what I was going through, had to bring one of her own nieces to help me. She was barely 10 or 11 years old, so she couldn't really do much.

I had to teach her how to do dishes and other little house chores like sweeping. My sister wouldn't even lift a broom to sweep anywhere.

As I was saying earlier, it was customary for me to receive and be startled by the chill of cold water on my bed. My brother in law would come by my room and pour cold water on me if I was sleeping past 5:30am in the morning. Mind you, he had to take his lunch to work, so I also needed to get up very early to prepare him something he would take to the office for lunch. Sometimes, he would tell me a night before or tell my sister what he would like to eat for lunch so we could have it ready.

What was very painful was not that I was going through all these things in my sister's house; but being awakened in the morning drenched in cold water-soaked clothes was humiliating. I had never experienced a thing like that before in my life. It was very terrifying, and I couldn't bear the pain. I would weep at nighttime when everyone was asleep to calm myself down.

What was even most painful was that my sister couldn't stop her husband from terrifying me!

Sometimes, if he didn't get hold of cold water, he would use a coaxial cable to whip me awake from sleep. I wondered what I did to deserve such treatments. Even though I was very good with the kids; I took very good care of them; why was he angry to the extent of whipping me? knowing that I barely got any reasonable sleep.

Let's talk about the food. I was doing most of the cooking. Initially when my brother-in-law judged that I added too much salt or a little less salt in the food, I was punished for that. My punishment was to add scoops of salts to the food, then sit at the dining table, and he would watch me eat the food, that was his way of telling me that I added too much or little salt to the food.

My God, I was only 14 or 15 years old. Before I lived with my sister, my mother and my brothers did most of the cooking. My chore was mainly doing dishes and doing some sweeping and house cleaning in the morning. It was my duty that dishes were ready for everyone to be served during meals. So, I didn't really know how to cook much. I mean my mother was a cook in my junior high school, she was a very great cook. I used to watch her cook at home.

I will also give my brother in law some credits, he thought me how to do some of the cooking. I guess that's why he would get so angry and make me eat food with piles of salts in it.

After a while of eating salty meals, I had to learn it.

I would literally pray to God to please make the salt right, so I don't have to eat salted food that day. God listened to my prayers and he answered them.

Furthermore, some nights, my brother-in-law would return home and request a fresh new meal apart from what he was served. Sometimes, it took up to 1 am in the morning to finish making his meals and serving him.

That's how some men live in Nigeria. I believe he deserved to eat whatever he wanted, but I just didn't believe I was the one responsible for his meals. I expected him to ask his wife for some of those services, serving his food and making other special meals at night. But my sister was usually not with it. Any day he made such requests, she just got up and walked into her bedroom to go to sleep.

Guess what? Once he made a mention of what he wanted to eat, it didn't matter what time it would take it to get the food ready, it was on me to do it. There was no other alternative.

By this time in my sister's house, I was already saturated with painful experiences. I guess I was more pained because my daddy had no clue of what was happening to me.

Letter to my Daddy

I started writing to my daddy through my mother; any time mom came by. I would write to my daddy enumerating my experiences.

Daddy wasn't coming by, and the phone system in Nigeria was the Nitel. Additionally, there was no GSM service in Nigeria then, so it was very had to communicate via the phone. Moreover, the few times that my daddy visited; I was in school. He visited during my school periods and I am not sure if he knew what was happening to me.

Most of the letters I wrote were taken away by my sister without my knowledge.

After few times, I asked my mother if she gave my letters to my daddy? She told me that my sister took them from her and would rip them into pieces after reading them. My mother was an accomplice.

I didn't know this, until my mother told me that none of those letters made it to my daddy.

Finally, I wrote one major letter, which had the narration of everything that happened to me, including my failing grades. One of the promises that my daddy ever made to me growing up was that I was his first-class baby, and because of that, he would make sure I got to any academic level I wanted. That's what gave me the drive, the audacity to proudly make good grades. When my daddy got my letter that Friday, the following Monday he was at my sister's house and was boiling in anger.

One of my brother in-law's relatives who was visiting them at that time told me he had never seen my father that angry before.

Unfortunately, I was in school, and my daddy waited for me because according to what I heard, he came to take me away from my sister's house.

However, my sister flipped the story, but she didn't know that I was told everything she told my father to calm him down and my daddy eventually got angry at me for being wayward. That was unimaginable.

Ok, when I returned home from school that day, this relative of my brother-in-law, was also furious at me, from everything that my sister had told them about me.

He told me that my father was so disappointed in me because of all the bad things my sister told him about me. This man told me he was shocked and didn't know I was this wayward. I was shocked and shaken. Apparently, my sister told my daddy that I was wayward and was running after boys, and that's why she decided to keep me at her house to monitor me closely. She also told him that I was at the verge of disgracing my family with an unwanted pregnancy.

I was told my sister brought out some of the clothes that her husband's niece gave to me and claimed to my dad that boys were buying clothes for me.

She also told my dad that after school dismissal, I usually went out with boys and returned home late from school. I heard so much accusations that had no single likeness of me.

Unfortunately, Mondays were the days I stayed back in school for extra classes to help me with my grades. She didn't tell my daddy that I was staying back in school to attend a lesson; rather she told my daddy that I usually wouldn't return home after school, though school closed at 1:30pm, I would normally come home at 3pm.

She told my daddy many things that made him get angry at me; and I was told my daddy waited for me until 3:30 pm before going back home. I had no clue where the lies came from, she knew very well that I had no boyfriend, and wouldn't even dare having one. Not only did I grow up as a very religious girl, my brothers always warned me that they would kill me if they ever found out that I had a boyfriend.

When I heard all those things, I broke down and wept. How can one's sister be this mean? I lost my only chance to recover academically. I just gave up on writing letters and decided to just finish my senior high school while living with her.

By the beginning of my last year as a senior in school, she had her third baby, a baby girl. This baby was my favorite among all of her kids. She was a very intelligent little girl and listened to me. She followed every instruction I gave her. I could tell the rest not to get their clothes dirty in school. The rest will have story to tell, but this one wouldn't.

I finished senior high school with beautiful grades. You know once I made up my mind that I was just going to finish up my high school while in her house. I devised a means of studying harder, mostly through the nights when everyone else was asleep and everywhere was quiet. I would start off crying, then wash my face and start reading. It was as if crying gave me energy enough to study. It was a way that I relieved stress or pressure, crying was therapeutic for me and still is.

When my senior school certificate (WAEC) results came out, I cleared all my papers. I believe the lowest grade was in mathematics, which was a pass.

Meanwhile, as I was still living with my sister, I started preparing for the university. I had to get registered for the joint admissions and matriculation board (JAMB) examinations, which was the sanctioning body for entrance into tertiary institutions in Nigeria. By this time, there was another niece to my brother-in-law who finished high school just like me, and she decided to come spend some time in my sister's house.

Rebecca was the biggest relief ever. She was hard working like me, so we would spin around the house cooking, cleanings and washing clothes. She always offered to do the washing since I mostly cooked.

This was when I got to breathe. Don't get me wrong, there were nieces to my brother in law who visited here and there, but they were like high class because they were raised in Lagos, a very big city in Nigeria. They really didn't want to do much in the house, though I didn't complain because I loved their company so much. They were so much fun to have around. We had free spiced dried meat called suyas, and other little treats here and there.

It is worthy to restate that the most part of my hardship came from the shock of the sudden change of school, the lies and ability to adapt to my failing grades in school. Those were nightmares. After I finished high school, I had a better adaptation. I was already used to many of the routines. And my sister's kids were growing so fast. While I was preparing for the university entrance exams, my sister had another baby girl. She was literally popping the babies out. She was very young and beautiful too.

I finished the JAMB exams and waited about three months for results. When the result returned back, my brother-in-law was very happy with my high score. Actually, after I received my Senior high school results, he was so impressed that he gave me some money to buy anything I wanted. He said he was worried how I was going to pass my exams seeing that I didn't have time to study. He didn't know that I studied when everyone was asleep. That's why I would wake up late in some of those days. If he bothered to know before pouring out the cold water on me, he would have known the reasons why I was waking up late.

He was so impressed with my results that he had to meet with the head of the department of the University to see how he could facilitate my getting into the university with my course of choice.

I gained admission to study Law at the University of Nigeria Enugu Campus. It's was a dream come true; a freedom finally attained.

My sister had suggested that I commute to school from her home, and I told her it would never happen. By this time, I was a little grown and heady too.

Christmas at home

For the first time that year, I was able to go home to spend the Christmas with my parents and my brothers. My brothers didn't really have a clue of what happened to me because I was numb and didn't really know how to tell those kinds of stories. My sister always had a way of convincing them that I was bad and didn't listen to her. I was so disciplined that I realized I had to be nice to myself and never make mistakes that will make my sister's lies about me becoming factual.

Christmas was fun, I got to see my friends and cousins, we had a lot of catching up to do.

After Christmas, I had gone to my cousin's house to celebrate the new year. Queendaline was my favorite cousin because we grew up together. She is my mother's baby sister's first daughter. It happened that I was few years older than her, so I was always protective of her as a big sister. She looked up to me, and we were very close. It was routine that she would visit our house to spend some time with me, and I would also do the same in their house, that's how we grew up.

Meeting Chimaroke

While returning from my cousin's house on the second of January, which was a walking trip with Queendaline, she was walking me home. I was stopped by a big Aunty who had gone to my parent's house first before she was told I was at my cousin's place.

This Auntie was a well-known politician and well respected, so when she went to my parents and requested them to release me to her for a few days, they didn't have any problem doing that.

Apparently, there was another politician who was running for a governorship election in few months; he needed a wife and a supposedly First Lady. This Auntie was the one assigned to help pick a good girl from my town for him. Chima wanted a woman from Ezza and I was the admirable one.

I grew up a beautiful young girl and of course every man would want a good girl that is well mannered and respectful, I fitted into all those qualifications.

My parents not in the know of what the plan was, agreed to let me go with her for just one night with the promise that she would bring me back the following day. She also told my parents that she had already discussed my being with her with my elder brother.

Trust the government drivers, the trip to Enugu was so fast. Enugu was where the seat of government was located.

Nonetheless, we went to my aunt's house first, because she also stayed in Enugu. Once we got to her house, I took a shower and she dressed me up nicely, she actually picked a nice dress from her closet. I didn't have a befitting dress that would have made me presentable to Chimaroke. Auntie dressed me up nicely and gave me one of her flat shoes. And her driver dropped me off at the suite where Chimaroke was staying; he wasn't the governor yet.

I stayed up for quite lots of hours, I was told he was out for a political campaign. He finally returned at about 2am in the morning. By this time, I was already tired and sicken, the air conditioner made the room so cold, I wasn't used to that.

When he came in, I was waiting in the living room, I greeted him, and he was happy to see me. He asked me to follow him to the room so we could be talking while he was settling down. I entered his room, and sat on the couch by the bed, and we started talking.

We had a very good conversation and I told him outrightly that I didn't really want to say no to my Aunt, but I wasn't ready for marriage. I was only 19yrs old and didn't want to get married before going to school. We talked at length, and he asked me about being his girlfriend, I said no as well.

A very gentleman, he didn't push me at all. He just called the driver to take me back to my aunt's house. I knew him as a gentleman and very polite, I didn't get to know any other side of him.

The next morning, Auntie took me back to my parents, and that was it.

I spent another week in the village with my parents before returning back to my sister's house to get ready for university.

The University of Nigeria Enugu Campus (UNEC)

UNEC was a very brilliant place to be associated with. First a Federal University where everyone was given a chance to excel. Both the rich, the middle class and poor had a chance to prove themselves. It's a prestigious university, and I was finally proud to be attending a great university, and also to study Law. I made friends, got to know different lifestyles, those who came to school to party and those like us who came in there to excel.

Matriculation happened after almost three months into school, there was a delay in getting people from the main campus to join us in the Enugu campus.

On the day of matriculation, I bumped into the big politician Auntie, and she was happy to see me in this prestigious school, her son was also matriculating with us.

We got talking, I gave her my new phone number, she stopped by my room in school to see me and her niece who was also my roommate.

Auntie didn't give up on me, so immediately she got home, she called Chimaroke who is now the new governor of the state. I am not sure what she told him, but I was told by my aunt that he was excited to hear about me, and he wanted to see me once again to see if I could just get to know him.

The Chase

I really didn't say no to Auntie, but I told her I will let her know when I will have time to see the governor. I was starting to hear stories about the governor, how he played around with some girls in my school, I didn't want to be tagged in school as one of those girls.

Auntie gave out my phone number to the governor who gave it to his personal assistant to try to find me.

His personal assistance (PA) never met me, so he didn't know what I looked like. He started searching for me all over the school. He called me few times and he said "Oga really wants to see you, please give him the chance "I told him I would once I get a little space. First semester Exam was fast approaching, and I didn't want any distractions.

The PA to the governor started driving to my school to search for me. He would wait outside my lecture hall, which was called Coscharis, to get hold of me.

This fateful Tuesday, he was determined because his boss really wanted to see me, and he came to the front of my hostel and packed his car there. Very embarrassing, many people knew who he was and were curious, he had the government vehicle with him. When he started asking around about me, my classmate came to my room and she yelled "Chioma, Frank is looking for you, so you know Frank?". I was the least person you would have thought to know the PA to the governor, because I was very quiet, and I didn't dress flashy. I didn't have plenty clothes to show off in school.

My sister would give me just about enough money to last me for two weeks, then I would return back to her house because I didn't have money. It was her way of control. I would get to her house on a Friday evening after school, then do some Saturday cleaning and cook enough soup and stew to last her for the week that I would be gone. Though by now, she had another little girl who joined my cousin Jacinta, to help with the house chores. My sister had no choice but to cook, because the two little girls could barely do great cooking. It was a relief for her to see me at her house at the given intervals, by now cooking had become my hubby.

Back to the governor's PA. I finally made it downstairs to speak to him. And after the begging, we agreed that he can pick me up that evening to go see the governor.

Government House Enugu

That evening, I dressed up very simple but nicely and I was picked up by Frank, the PA to the governor. When I got to the palace of the governor, he was all excited. He lifted me up and gave me a kiss, I became uncomfortable and he noticed. He apologized and told me how he has been looking for me after the first time he saw me. My Auntie didn't have my phone number, and she didn't want my sister to know that the governor was interested in me.

It was as if we had known each other for a long time, he was comfortable enough to tell me many things. And he said he was traveling the following weekend to London and he would want me to come with him, that's why he was desperate to find me so they could get me a passport and visa.

I was flabbergasted, I was flattered, but something in me told me nope. And I told him I wasn't ready. He started asking me personal questions like if I had a boyfriend in school? I told him the truth, I had none and he wanted to know if I was still a virgin, I said yes.

He said I must marry him, he pleaded with me. He told me he would pamper me and make sure I was comfortable.

For the London trip, I told him I had exams that date and wouldn't be able to make it.

He wanted to know who my professor was? and he told me that if I became his wife, they would come to lecture me at home. Scariest thing ever, did he know what I just escaped from?

We spoke at length; we were like old friends. I was becoming a little comfortable with him.

After few hours of talking with the governor, he told his PA to drop me off, and to find out my actual room number.

I was more comfortable with his PA, so I told him that I wouldn't make it for the London trip, and he shouldn't bother looking for me. That evening when he dropped me off, he gave me a bundle of money, he said Oga (the governor) said I should give you some money. I counted it and it was twenty-five thousand Naira. I don't remember ever touching that kind of money.

My fear about the governor grew stronger when I heard some rumors that he was using virgin girls for occultic rituals.

After he returned from his trip, he told his PA to pick me up that he wanted to see me. This time around in his office, he just barely got into his office. And I agreed to go see him, but I told the PA when he called me that I was finishing up a lecture at 12 noon and that I have another one at 2 pm. He offered to pick me up briefly after my afternoon lecture and he would make sure I made it on time for the late afternoon lecture.

Even though I told him to pick me up at the hostel, he was by my lecture hall before my class was finished that afternoon. Now everyone noticed I was the girl who got picked up, but they didn't know if I was dating Frank the PA or the Governor. I didn't tell anyone anything except my roommates.

When I got to his office, I went pass the protocol and went pass hundreds of people that were waiting to see the governor.

I got into his office, and he told me to sit on his laps around his round table. What did I do, I obeyed him; At this point, I didn't want to hurt his feelings. And we talked and he wanted me to return in the evening to his palace. According to him for what he bought for me from London. I agreed to return, but when I got into PA's car, I started crying. And he was shocked, he was worried to hear what was making me cry. I told him my story and I told him that I really don't want Oga. I told him that I wasn't ready for this kind of relationship. I told him I was afraid of Oga.

This PA was my life saver, he told me that Oga doesn't really associate with girls, and he has noticed that he really likes me, and this is why he tries to get me whenever Oga asks for me.

He told me that the opportunity I have is what many girls from my school are looking for.

I told him I wasn't interested. And we agreed that he would advise Oga to leave me alone that I was going through some tough times emotionally.

That was the last time he came to pick me up. It was like a divine intervention. An answered prayer. I really was so scared of him, the rumors of girls disappearing, and some girls being used for rituals was always flying around; I was terrified.

CHAPTER FOUR

The New Covenant Family (NCF)-UNEC

T HE New covenant family was the name which the church fellowship
was known at the campus stage, before the church grew to became
Dominion City.

My roommate Chilee in UNEC was attending this NCF school fellowship
and I admired her so much because she was so dedicated to it. I was also a
very dedicated Catholic and while she would wake up in the morning to
attend morning prayers, I would also wake up to attend morning masses
at Saint Mulumba, the school catholic church.

There were incidents where students going for morning masses were
harassed by unknown cult boys. It deterred many of us who were faithful
in attending morning masses. While Chilee would wake up to attend her
morning prayers, I would be up and trying to pray in the room. One day
Chilee asked me to attend prayers with her since her Fellowship was close
to the school hostel and in a safer environment.

You know as a Catholic, I was very weary of those who called themselves
born again Christians because I didn't speak in tongues and didn't really
believe in it. Anything that would make you attend a church where loud
noises were made, my mother condemned.

This was the case even from my childhood, I used to get in deep trouble
because I sneaked out to attend a midweek service with our neighbors
who attended Assemblies of God Church close to our house.

My mother didn't like them because they were always trying to get us to believe that we were not true Christians since we prayed through Mary by counting the rosary beads. Now, I totally see what they were trying to say, but back in the days, my mother was so angry to hear them talk about the rosary.

When my roommate started to invite me to her church fellowship, I frowned at it initially because I didn't want to disrespect my mother.

After few invites and when the incidents of cult boys harassing girls around the road that led to the Catholic Church in school increasing, I decided to give Chilee's school fellowship a try.

I attended one Sunday evening fellowship, and I liked it. Within the week, I attended the morning prayer. I didn't really enjoy it because all they did in most of the service was praying in tongues. Since I wasn't speaking in tongues, it was boring to me. Though I admired how everyone prayed in different tongues even though it was loud and a kind of noisy to me.

Nonetheless, during one of the Sunday evening services, one of the co-pastors, Ijeoma Abana (Pastor IJ) called out people who didn't speak in tongues to get them filled with the Holy Spirit.

Oh! Before this encounter, the first time I attended the Sunday evening service something interesting happened. After the word, the pastor, David Odeta called out people who would want to give their lives to Christ. I wasn't sure what to make out of it, I knew I had experienced Jesus Christ and I always prayed to him and believed in him. Just to make sure I didn't miss anything; I walked forward and gave my life again to Jesus Christ.

After that prayer of salvation, I became more joyous about attending this fellowship more and more. It was as if I was initiated into Christ. This Joy was what made me long to learn how to speak in tongues.

When Pastor IJ made the announcement for people who were interested in receiving the gift of the Holy Spirit by speaking in new tongues to step forward, I volunteered to be prayed for.

She told us what to do and that we could receive it by faith, I just did what I was told to do. The head pastor laid hands on us and that was it. I felt different, but my faith was not that strong, though I continued to believe.

We were told by the pastors to always pray in tongues any time we wanted to pray.

I started practicing what I was taught until one faithful Sunday morning, I decided to attend the main Church with them in town. Sunday morning I still attended masses at Catholic Church, then Sunday evening I would attend fellowship at NCF.

So that Sunday morning I decided to go for a special service outside school, in the city.

There, I met with the presence of God. The head pastor, David Ogbueli's teaching was something I never heard before. I was intrigued and engrossed in his teaching until the end of the service. Did he not talk about the Holy Spirit that day, and his manifestations? I really felt something extraordinary that day. On my way home that very day, I decided to put into practice what the man of God taught us. I asked the Holy Spirit that I was too hungry and that I would really want to eat Rice and Stew for lunch, though I had no food in my hostel. And I actually asked him to provide me with Rice and Stew by the time I get back to school. I was in a bus when I said these things.

When I got into school, I had already forgotten what I asked the Holy Spirit for until my roommate and friend Chinwe Udeh told me that her sister visited her from town, and she brought some Rice and Stew for us.

Did we not dance like two crazy people? We did because we were actually out of food that weekend, and we planned to go to the market on Monday if we could access the bank. We ran out of cash too. We didn't have like the swipe debit cards then. You would normally need to go into the bank to withdraw money from the teller if you wanted money from the bank.

And when I sat to eat the food, I was reminded of my prayer, and I started crying. My friend thought I was just emotional because I was so hungry, but I told her that I prayed a prayer that God should provide me rice and stew for lunch, and God did.

That changed the way I viewed God, I realized I could actually talk to God and get a response from him. Now, I became more conscious of my lifestyle, I didn't want to hurt God's feelings. Pastor Ogbueli had mentioned in his teachings on the Holy Spirit that holy spirit is a person that you could hurt his feelings.

This was how my life totally changed. Before I knew it, I could pray in a different tongue. I didn't know when exactly it happened, I just realized that one day I wanted to pray during the weekly morning prayers, and I started to pray in tongues.

As time passed, I totally stopped going to the Catholic Church, I wanted more on Sunday mornings. I craved to hear Pastor David Ogbueli's teachings. It was so fresh from heaven. And everything he said worked for me, God was drawing me to himself. Pastor David Ogbueli is still a stream of water, he has so much wisdom of the word of God.

Then, I started attending leadership trainings, foundation school courses, the disciple school and school of ministry. I grew in that fellowship, and actually had a leadership position.

Student Church Bus

Suddenly, there was a need for a church bus. The number of students attending Sunday morning services in the city increased, and it was beginning to cost the fellowship quite much to transport everyone to the city on a Sunday morning.

We started raising funds for a new student bus. Suddenly, I remembered the Governor, I was unsure if I wanted to bother him though, but the pressure was on in my heart, and I continued to hear in my heart that I could do something about it. Then I didn't understand why I was so troubled, but now I do, it was my friend the Holy Spirit who wanted me to help the Church raise the money.

After a few weeks of trying to raise the money for the bus, we were not anywhere close to the funds needed for the bus. I decided to approach my school fellowship pastor, David Odeta. I told him that I know someone who could help us with the money. I told him about the governor, and I wanted him to pray for me, and I told him first thing Monday morning I was going to go to his office and ask him for the funds.

He was shocked, but he agreed to pray for me about the trip for Monday morning.

After the prayers, I got ready and went to the government house.

I got to the gate and the security stopped me because I took a taxi. Back in the days, the PA to the governor would pick me up. When I got to the gate, I told the security I was coming to see Frank, the PA to the governor. He radioed the PA and told him my name; I could hear him telling them to let me in. When I got to his office, I told him I had a project in school that I needed Oga's assistance in completing. He said hmm, you have started again Chioma! We laughed about it and called Oga's office and told him I was in his office and that I wanted to see him. Oga had some elder statesmen meetings and there were group of chiefs in his reception waiting to see him. He told PA to bring me into his office before the meeting.

Boom! I walked past these men some of them older than my grandpa into the governor's office.

He was so excited to see me, and I was too. For some reason, I realized that I missed talking with him, we were beginning to develop some kind of friendship, but I didn't want it to progress, I was too afraid.

We spent few minutes talking, then I told him I needed financial help with a project in school and he told me it's not a problem. He asked how much? I told him fifty thousand Naira. He said it was ok, he called his PA in and told him to drop me off at school and told him to give me whatever I needed.

It was a miracle, the prayer worked. I didn't want him asking me out again, so that prayer actually worked.

Before 12 noon, I was back in school with a bundle of money we needed in fellowship to purchase the bus. After I changed into my normal clothes, I took a bike down to my pastor's house. Yes, my pastor Odeta was also a student in school. He was shocked to see me back so soon, he thought it didn't work. Once I got into his room, I took the bundle of money and handed it to him.

He stared at me for quite a bit, he said we have someone like you in this fellowship, and we have been suffering? We laughed about it and I left to get back to my afternoon lectures.

Camp meetings

Church fellowship became my main attraction in school, I participated more and more.

Easter holidays weekends were special weekends, because of the retreat no one wanted to miss. It was always a time of encounters, where great men and women of God in Nigeria and outside Nigeria were invited to spend time with the whole Church family.

It was an Easter retreat that started on Thursday Evening and lasted until Sunday and, it was a power packed conference.

That particular Easter of 2001, I decided to stay back in school because the camp meeting venue was at my school hall.

I was in big trouble, my sister expected me at her house for Easter, but I was in school. I had gone to her office to inform her that I will be spending the Easter in school because of the fellowship. She was furious, she called my brothers and told on me. She knew something was changed about me, but she didn't believe me. She thought maybe I had followed a boyfriend home for the holiday.

On Easter Saturday, she sent one of my big brothers, Okechukwu to come check if I was in school. He came and actually enjoyed part of the Church service. He wanted me to follow him home, but I was too passionate of my newfound love, I didn't care if I got into troubles chasing after Jesus.

After the camp meeting, I went back to my hometown to see my parents because I didn't want to have any form of argument with my sister.

My parents were already told that I have become rebellious because I now attend a Pentecostal church. My parents didn't really take any of those complaints serious, they were in denial. They knew how I participated in Catholic Church and I was a member of many groups within the Catholic Church family.

The American Visa Lottery

My brother in law's niece who lived in America returned home for her sister's wedding that same Easter period. After the wedding, she was returning back to the USA, and she decided she would play the Visa lottery for everyone including her family members. She collected everyone's photos for the application. Unfortunately, I didn't have any photos available, and I was not really interested because at that point, I didn't see myself going to America.

The visa lottery is a program from USA to other countries. The lottery is administered by the United States Department of States.

This program Makes available 55,000 immigrant visas annually. It aims to diversify the immigrant population in the United States, by selecting applicants from countries with low numbers of immigrants in the USA.

She insisted she wanted my photos and offered for the driver who drove her around to drive me to my school hostel to pick up some passport photos in school. I had plenty of them that I used for forms in the school.

We got to my school, and I picked up two passport photos and handed them to her. She was already heading back to the USA, so once I gave her the passport photos she headed to the airport.

After about six months, she called from the USA. She said that, out of all the many people whose names were entered for the visa lottery applications, my name returned back successful. I didn't know what that meant, I was confused at that point because I was just finishing my third year as a law student, and still needed two more years to complete my program.

So, I just told my sister that I wasn't interested, because I wouldn't want to leave school. I have always loved school and I didn't want anything that would disrupt my schooling. I moved on and continued with school.

During Christmas of 2001, all my brothers were around, and the visa lottery was a topic of discussion. Many of my cousins who heard about it, made it a big deal and were happy for me. I didn't understand why they were so happy. Not like I didn't like the USA, I just didn't picture myself in the USA, so it wasn't exciting me like others who had fantasies about America.

After I saw the level of excitement in my brothers and family members, I started thinking about it, but was still undecided.

By January 2002, I needed to start the Visa lottery processing. This warranted frequent traveling to Lagos where the American Consulate was located.

At the time that all the processes were completed, and it was already October. Since I was in school, I took my time to do everything. I waited for the last minutes to get things back to the consular in Lagos. More like I wasn't sure if I really wanted to go to the USA.

Since, my family agreed that I should go through the visa processing and at least have my visa ready in case I changed my mind.

Meeting my husband

In the process of seeking my United States immigrant visa in Lagos, my cousin Queendaline, tried to hook me up with her fiancé's friend called Chris. Chris lived in Lagos, very close to the US Consulate.

Chris had returned home during Easter holiday to see me and perhaps get acquainted. But I spent that period in the church camp meeting retreat, so he wasn't able to see me before returning to Lagos.

In the process of securing my visa in Lagos, after few pressures from my cousin's fiancé Jeff to allow his friend to call me. I agreed and allowed Jeff to give him my phone number.

He called me the next day, and we agreed to meet on a Saturday. At this time, I stayed with my brother in law's older niece.

My brother in law's older niece was very nice to me, so I told her about Chris, and how he wanted to pick me up from her house on Saturday. She said I have to make sure I returned back to the house by 5 o'clock in the evening before her husband returned home.

Though I was in the University and at my age I had no serious boyfriend, because I was a born-again Christian and seriously involved in church. Additionally, my pastor in school had warned us about being unequally yoked with unbelievers.

I had few unserious relationships here and there. You know once you are not willing to have sex with a man, they don't commit. So, some of the guys who were interested in me were just there and I didn't really want anything from them. I wanted a man that I would date then marry, not a fling.

I called Chris and told him he could pick me up that Saturday, but he must bring me back to Auntie Angela's house by 5 o'clock in the evening.

Saturday by 12 noon, he picked me up, and we went to Victoria Garden City (VGC). Yes, he lived in VGC, he was doing very well in Lagos, a computer engineer, also had his own business.

He showed me around Lekki, which VGC was situated and we had some great talking. By 3 o'clock in the afternoon, we were on our way back to Akoka where Auntie Angela lived. He didn't want to disappoint her, so he behaved himself.

With Chris, it was love at first sight, I liked him immediately and he felt the same way too. It was as if we knew each other for years. Though he knew my brothers and my sister, but I didn't really know him.

We continued to talk through the weekend, and on Monday morning he picked me up at a Junction to take me to Lekki where I had my medical screenings. And once I was done, I called him, and he picked me up back to Akoka. He had a gift for me, a new cell phone. I had one of those cheap phones, and he probably didn't like it. He took my old phone and removed the SIM card and connected it to the new phone. Hmm, he created a very intelligent impression.

The next morning, I left back for school. On my way through the eight hours journey, all I did was think about Chris. I was happy and he was happier.

After few weeks, it was time to go back for my visa. This time, we decided I should stay in VGC Lekki; Auntie Angela's house was almost two hours away from the Consulate, because of the usual Lagos morning traffic.

I didn't tell my sister my decision, she thought I was going to stay with her husband's niece Auntie Angela as usual.

When I got to Lagos, Chris picked me at Ekene Dili Chukwu Motor park terminal in Yaba. And I called Auntie Angela and told her that I was going to stay at my girlfriend's parents' house who lived closer to the Consulate. She said it was ok, and she called her Uncle, my sister's husband to let him know I wasn't staying at her house.

Next thing at 11 pm at night, my phone rang, and it was my Military brother, the one and only brother you never want to make angry.

He was so furious, yelling about the decision I made to stay somewhere else. I got into trouble, and I was feverish that night. Chris was so shocked to see me suddenly develop fever just from a phone call. I told him that I needed to go back to Akoka that night, which was what my brother told me to do. Chris said he wasn't going to do that. I was so afraid of my brother, he has never hit me, because I always behaved myself. Everyone in my city knew who my brothers were, so they really never wanted anything to do with me if not marriage.

When I told Chris that I need him to drop me off that night, he told me he will deal with the consequences, and that it would never happen.

I stayed with him that period and returned back to school after few days of completing what I was in Lagos to do.

I was summoned to come home to my sister's house and unfortunately my brother had something to do in Enugu, and he stopped by to greet my sister when all these things were happening. I wasn't so unlucky. He didn't hit me, but he was very mad at me.

Chris had taken me shopping that weekend in Lagos, he gave me the strength to pretend as if I wasn't in trouble, but I was so troubled.

Chris didn't like my sandals because they were cheap sandals compared to his standard. He took me to a shop where they sold Italian shoes and bought a very nice pair of sandals for me. The guy who owned the shop, gave me another pair, he said Chris was his good customer, and I must be important to him, he never really brought any woman to his shop. I got a free pair of sandals from the guy.

Chris told me he didn't want me for a girlfriend because there were plenty of them in Lagos. He wanted me to be his wife. We started talking marriage right from the very first time he picked me up from Auntie Angela's house.

That was the end of hardship for me; Chris literally turned things around for me, I didn't ask for money. He just gave me money that I was afraid to spend. I remember one time I visited from school; I didn't have to tell anyone what I was doing anymore. I summoned that courage to get to really date Chris. When I visited, he gave me a bundle of money, same amount that the Governor gave me for my school bus. He wanted me to buy food stuff for cooking. I became scared of this guy. I said, I didn't know what he did to get that kind of money. I took about few notes from the bundle and left the rest on the table in his bedroom.

I didn't really have to cook anything for Chris, we ate at the restaurant in VGC. I was so spoiled by this guy; I was like where were you all these years man?

From the time I met him until I left Nigeria, I never lacked anything. He would call me up to tell me he just put some money in my school account for my hair. He loved nails, so I started getting myself packaged.

My problem started when I visited my sister, and she saw that I have become different. She asked me about the sandals, the phone. She is my only sister, so I told her the truth how I met Chris and how he said he wants me as a wife.

My sister's reaction shocked me, I was falling in love and I was happy, I had expected her to give me a listening ear as a sister; I wish I had a better relationship with my sister.

She told me outrightly that I can't marry Chris. My sister had her own plans for me. I was so shocked to my bones. That was the beginning of my marital nightmares.

In October 2002, I visited Lagos, and since I was in school, I didn't really tell anyone when my appointments at the consulate was. I just told Chris everything, and he would arrange and pick me up at the bus terminal, and I would stay with him then return back to school.

Back in school, my pastor with his spiritual eyes noticed some changes, though he knew I was frequently going to Lagos because of my visa. But he told me he couldn't see that glowing light he used to see around me.

Chris was a Catholic who didn't really believe in Pentecostal churches. He saw them as frauds. I didn't try to convince him; I knew the consequences of getting married to a man who was drinking a lot. One of the concerns I had about him was his drinking habits. He would drink bottles of beer when we visited restaurant and suya places. He noticed I was uncomfortable, because I would be quiet and not speak to him. He watched my face a lot, he still does.

He minimized his drinking whenever he was with me.

My pastor was disappointed in me when I told him about Chris. He wanted me to be married to someone who had my kind of spiritual background, by then I had already made up my mind to be with Chris.

Suddenly, there was a strike by the lecturers in the university, and we had to leave school. I stayed with my sister, and it was tough because I didn't have any excuse to go to Lagos after I received my Visa in October. In November, Chris had to come down to the East; Lagos was located in the

Western part of Nigeria, While Enugu was located in the Eastern part. I had already told my sister I was going home to see my parents. So, Chris picked me up and we went down to Abakaliki.

We visited his mom and some of his siblings, while I stayed at my cousin's Queendaline.

We were happy. After one week, Chris had to go back to work, he dropped me off at my sister's house then went back to Lagos.

By December, I spoke to my sister again about him, she insisted that I wasn't going to marry Chris. She told me, since I was traveling by next year, I was better off with an American husband. My sister just speaks with too much authority regarding my choice for a husband. Her leverage over my life was really long and my memories living with her was tainted. In truth, those were experiences I choose not to remember. Nonetheless, to me, she was just joking too much. I was amazed to hear my sister trying to decide who I married, it just made me mad.

I totally stopped talking to her about it, and I started talking to my mother. My mom was excited for me, at least I have never mentioned anyone to her before, so she told me it would be a great idea since we both come from the same state, and my father knew his father very well.

Chris didn't want to rush anything, he wanted me to travel and return again to see if I really wanted him.

The only concern I had about him was that I couldn't trust him with women and his drinking. Though I never really saw him with any woman, some hidden characteristics just made me suspect something was wrong. He would sometimes ignore his call or go out of my sight to pick up a call.

I was very sensitive, so I noticed those traits and I didn't need anyone to tell me what they were.

Since I was very close to God, I started asking God to intervene in Chris's life. I wanted him to become born again like me. At this point, I was so blown away by him. I had a prayer partner and we used to go up to the mountains to pray. I started going up to the mountains with him, strictly to pray for Chris. I would spend hours on my knees just asking God for one thing, to change Chris's life.

By January 2003, I had about two months for my visa to expire. My visa was due to expire on April 14th, 2003. Meaning if I didn't get into the USA by that date, I would have forfeited my visa. So, with me being in my fourth year, and just one more year to finish law school, I was concerned. My brothers agreed that I would just go into the USA, get my green card then return back to continue with school.

Farewell Prayers

When it was concluded that I had to leave for Lagos, my sister being a faithful member of the Adoration Ministries Enugu, told the Priest in Charge of the ministry who was well known for his Holy Ghost filled services.

The last Sunday before I left for Lagos, there was a thanksgiving service conducted in the Church. And during the benediction, the Priest called me out with my brother to anoint and pray for us. It was such a privilege since he didn't do that a lot. I was blessed and ready to go to the USA.

Devilish Encounter

The following Monday morning, my sister told my brother to take me to a woman who did prayers for her in order for the woman to lay hands on me and pray for me.

I didn't want to do that since I was already prayed for and blessed by the priest. I told my sister that I was good to go after the blessings I received from the priest.

She insisted, and because I didn't want any more troubles from her, I agreed to go with my brothers. Two of them, Ike and Tony.

When we got there, this woman started her ministrations as they call it. She danced around with the girls that worked with her in her altar.

She called me out from where I was sitting, I took off my shoes as you were not allowed to wear shoes into her altar.

Suddenly she started shouting at me saying, you are possessed! you are possessed! And I turned to her in dismay. I told her she didn't know what she was talking about. I told her that I am a born again and Holy Ghost filled, I couldn't be possessed. Immediately she slapped me three times, and she told me to shut up, and told the girls who were dancing around with her to restrain me. I was shaking and looking at my brothers to rescue me, but they were still in shock. And watching this woman, she took water from the kettle that was on her altar and forced it into my mouth. I was struggling with her and the two other ladies who were restraining me. To avoid further embarrassment and the slaps, I had a drink of the water from the dirty kettle.

After that, she told my brothers she wanted to give me a message privately with them.

I was so humiliated and angry at the same time. When we went into her house for the message, which was around the corner from the place of prayer. She started telling me that there is a man that she saw while praying for me, she said this man was waiting for me, this man lives in the USA and would want to get married to me as soon as he sets his eyes on me.

Oh my! I wasn't interested in that kind of message, so I told her immediately that I already have someone I was dating and that we were talking about marriage.

She told me to forget about the guy in Lagos, he is not your husband she said. I totally looked at her as a joke. I was too angry for the water she forced into my mouth. I told my brothers I was ready to leave.

When I got home that evening, I was weakened, I felt something was very wrong. Did my sister tell this woman to manipulate me this way, or is there more to this act? I couldn't eat the whole night because I was so weak.

Very early in the morning, around 6 am, I saw a lizard, an agama lizard which was on the floor of my room staring at me. This lizard pooped on the floor, but I was still so weak to move. Immediately I tried to lift my body out of the bed, the lizard jumped on my waist, while I laid on the bed and on my belly. I jumped up but didn't see the lizard anymore. I looked for this lizard everywhere in the room, and the poop, I didn't see anything. The next day being Tuesday morning, my sister wanted me to return back to the woman because she wanted to see me again. When I got there, I told her what happened to me, and she said it was ok, I should not worry about it. She told me that the lizard would have been a hinderance during my journey in the USA, but the prayers destroyed everything. I was not convinced with what she said, but I was not ready to continue to argue with such a mean hearted personality.

The next evening, being Wednesday, a day for Adoration in the Adoration Ministries Enugu, I went to see the Holy Ghost priest to tell him what happened to me. I couldn't meet him because he was so busy. Earlier on, I had told my sister what happened to me, how that woman slapped me three times, and poured water from a dirty kettle into my mouth. And that a lizard jumped on my waist. She laughed about it and told me that's how the woman conducts deliverance.

I wondered what had happened to my sister, she was really a stranger to relate to. I just elated to be quiet because I didn't want any troubles.

Thursday morning, I left for Lagos. My mother and father came to my sister's house to bless me and to bid me good-bye.

On April 12, 2003, I left for the USA via Lagos international Airport. My brothers paid for my ticket and gave me $1000 just to enable me spend time until I get my green card. That was the initial plan.

CHAPTER FIVE

The USA

I ENTERED THE USA ON APRIL 14, 2003, a very memorable day. I can still remember my KLM flight from Nigeria with a stop at Amsterdam then to Newark International Airport.

I was picked up by my brother in-law's niece. I was very happy to meet her again after a few years. You know when I lived with my sister, she also stayed at my sister's house for a few years. She actually studied at UNEC and left for the USA when she got married to her husband. When she was at my sister's house, we were very close. I had a closer relationship with her than my sister. She was very nice to me. So, it's was encouraging when my sister told me that I will be staying at her house.

Somerset

Somerset was the name of the city where I found myself and it was spring, so the weather was a bit cold. For me, it was a freezing cold, especially at night, but I survived the spring season anyway. Summer was the weather I longed for because I was told it was a warm weather. Summer came, and the parties started. We had block parties and attended Nigerian gatherings almost every weekend.

You know back in Nigeria, I hardly attended parties, so it was something very different for me, getting to meet and know people.

The people I stayed at their house were very sociable. They had friends who came over to their house almost every weekend. I did most of the cooking because cooking had become a hubby for me. And since I was actually at home most of the time, I did nothing but cook and clean.

The Twist

My trouble started when I waited and waited for my green card to come through the mail. I was told by the immigration officer that I cannot call or come to the immigration office until after 6 months if I don't receive my green card. There was no way I could leave the USA back to Nigeria without my green card, and I didn't defer my law program in UNEC. I was hoping that before the strike was over, I would have picked up my green card and gone back. It is worthy of mention that lecturers in Nigerian colleges were always on strike action against the government, for wage and conditions of service-related issues.

After three months, I called my roommate and my friend Chinwe Udeh to help me defer my schooling for six months. I sent her all the information she needed to get it done, and it was done.

The first Monday morning after the sixth month, I was at the immigration office. When they looked in their system, I was told that the people who processed my application moved from where they lived. My green card was mailed to their old address and was returned back to the Department of Immigrations.

Apparently, federal mails are not forwarded, so if the postmaster was unable to deliver it, he simply returned it back. And the people that I stayed with moved from their previous city to a new one but forgot to notify the federal mailing system of their new address.

That alone put me in a very tight position. It took another two months before I got my green card. Anyway, one thing led to another and my brothers told me there was no need rushing back to Nigeria, I should try to see what else I could get done in the USA.

The advice

My brother in law's niece advised me on the few career choices that I had. Notably, going to a nursing school which my lead me to becoming a nurse, of which I frowned at the suggestion or pursuing other career trajectories through the courses I choose in school.

However, after weighing in on many of my options, I needed to get a driver's license first and a car, then a job before school.

Everything was falling into place, until after one year and three months, I was told by the people that I stayed with that it was time for me to move on and find a place of my own and shortly, I will get to the reason why she wanted me to move on.

Firstly, I never expected a thing like that, I was shocked to my bones. I considered many options including returning back to Nigeria, but by this time I had already started taking classes at a community college and thus returning to Nigeria was not palatable.

Furthermore, it is worthy of mention that by this time, I had a home health job which paid reasonably compared to when I worked in KFC and then Walmart.

Even though the home health job paid me better, I also had a car that I was basically spending all my money on. My brother in law's niece had given me her old car because she bought a new one. The car was one of the best things that happened to me as of then, it helped me get out of the house and try to do things for myself.

Oh! You remember Chris, he called me every day and I also was so in love, so I spent my money on calling cards to Nigeria. After I ramped up their phone bills within two months of being at their house. I was mostly at home by myself or some days that my brother in law's niece's five-year-old son didn't go to school, he stayed with me; I helped her with babysitting.

So, the first few months, I had no clue that I couldn't use the phone to call Chris. I would call him, and he would call me back immediately. By the first two months, I had already costed them few hundred of dollars in phone bills.

This actually made her husband mad, and it was very understandable. I was told how it worked that I needed to buy prepaid cards to call Nigeria. Remember I had $1000 with me, so I had money to spend on calling cards.

Nigerian Church

Immediately I started driving, I was hardly at home. I moved from one place to another, job hunting being part of it. And on one of those occasions, I met Makala. She was a very friendly person and gave me lots of information regarding the kind of job I was looking for.

Additionally, she was attending a Nigerian church and since I was a Nigerian who just got to the USA, she wanted to introduce me to her Nigerian Church family.

Catholic Church in USA is very different to Nigeria Catholic Church. In Nigeria, there were many celebrations that made the church very lively. In my opinion, Catholic Church Services at Somerset was very quiet, and only lasted for one hour. So, when Makala told me about the Nigerian Church, I was very interested to hear more. I gave her my phone number and told her to contact me on Sunday morning.

Nonetheless, after two weeks of turning her down, I decided to try her Nigerian Church out. Makala had a young daughter and didn't drive, so I offered to pick her up that Sunday morning.

Meeting the Pastor

After the church service, everyone came to say hi to me and to welcome me to the church. They were so friendly and welcoming, I felt at home. That was how I became a member of the church. You know, once I felt comfortable, I became very dedicated to the church services.

Then the pastor asked me to join the ushering department since that was the department I worked in back in Nigeria.

I was happy and enthusiastic about serving and the head Usher; Sumbo

51

became a very close friend. After joining the church, it was as if my prayer life began coming back to life.

Friday nights were prayer vigils, which started at 12 midnight and ended at 3AM in the morning.

By this time, the people I stayed with were no longer happy with me because I attended a different church; and the night vigils was not an idea they liked.

In August of 2004, I was told by the lady I lived with that her husband wants me to move on with my life. She said that I was becoming a nuisance. The only way to remain at their house was if I stopped attending the night vigils on Friday nights.

I apologized to them, and since I was very close to the lady, I tried to find out what exactly I did wrong. She said her husband complained that I was always in my room when they had guests and the churching was becoming too much.

Ok, let me get into the details. You remember that I had already agreed to be Chris's wife before I came to the USA, the point was that apparently, there were some of their friends who wanted to get to know me, but I was not entertaining their presence. I was in love with Chris, and I didn't care for any other man.

The pressure was still on from my sister in Nigeria to get into a relationship in the USA and try to forget about Chris.

And Chris didn't make it easy for me either and there was a point he threatened he didn't want the relationship anymore. We were fighting quite often because I wanted to hear from him more often, it was apparent that we had time difference issues. He was calling so late at night and it wasn't helping. My life was so complicated, and I was so confused with the pressures here and from Nigeria.

Meeting Sam

The car my brother in law's niece gave to me was draining me financially. I spent almost all my money on it. Every week, there was always something wrong immediately I got paid at work. Oh yes, I got a home health aide job after the training, and I was lucky to be assigned to little kids at their homes. So, I was making reasonable amount of money weekly, and I was in turn spending the money on the car and gas.

On one of those occasions, I went to fix my car at a Nigerian car shop in New Brunswick, very close to Somerset. There was this guy, very good looking, was just sitting with the guy that usually fixes my car.

When I dropped off my car, the mechanic told me it would take few hours, and he would call me back once he was done. He told me I could either take a taxi or allow his friend sitting beside him to drop me off since he was going to Somerset. The coincidence was just too good to be true. I guess that's life and it creates circumstances that can set one up, especially if the devil is interested in one.

I was uncomfortable to allow a stranger, drop me off, so I thought about taking a taxi.

Nonetheless, Sam was the guy's name that was sitting with the mechanic and he told me I shouldn't be afraid that he was actually going to Somerset. Anyway, they were my Nigerian people, so I felt a little comfortable riding with him after all.

When I got into his BMW X5, it felt different from my car. I have always wanted good things; I just didn't want to do wrong things to have good things.

Sam dropped me off at home, it was in the afternoon so, no one was home. And he wanted my number because while I was riding with him, he told me he would pick me up once the mechanic was done so I can go get my car.

He was very nice to me, though I hesitated, but I gave him my number. He called the mechanic to let him know when he was done fixing my car, and he was going to pick me up. I believe it was all a set-up, because

I have been going to this mechanic for some time now, I wasn't sure how this guy just appeared from nowhere and was so nice to me. It was all programmed.

Afterward, I picked up my car and went home. Now, Sam knows where I live, and has my number. After few days, he called to find out how the car was doing. That was how I started talking to him. Just friendly talk. After few weeks, Sam wanted to come around to see me. Since I was very close to the lady that I stayed in her house, I told her everything. There was nothing happening between me and Chris that she didn't know. And when Chris started missing my calls, I was devastated, but I was also ready to move on since my sister didn't approve of him anyway. So, few days would go by and I wouldn't hear from Chris. I started talking to Sam more often, we would chat on the phone few minutes every day. He was very funny, so he made me laugh a lot. I was comforting myself with his phone calls. I told everyone else who seemed to like me about a guy called Chris back in Nigeria, and how I wasn't interested in any relationship. So, when I met Sam, he didn't ask me, and I didn't bother to tell him anything.

Sam was into computers like Chris, so he worked from home most times. He would call me while working from home and we would chat for a long time. I don't remember what we used to talk about, but nothing serious.

When Sam insisted, he wanted to come see me since I wasn't agreeing to visiting him, I told my brother in-law's niece. She was excited shockingly and she told me Sam can visit if he wanted. She told me to invite him over for Christmas dinner.

And I was happy, and I called him and told him. He was so excited.

At Christmas dinner, he was there. We ate and after talking with my uncle as I would call her husband, I walked him to his car.

Sam made a comment, he said my Uncle was watching him from the glass door upstairs. I brushed it aside that it didn't matter.

By midnight, I was called downstairs by my uncle and his wife. He started by saying that he had told me back in August that I was going to move by December this year, and he said he wanted me out of his house by the

31st of December which was like a week's time. I didn't beg and I didn't apologize like I did back in August. I told him it was ok by me. I went to my room, and I called Sam, and I told him that he just got me in trouble.

Sam told me I could come stay with him, but I knew that I would rather go back to Nigeria than live my life like that.

I started hunting for an apartment for rent, maybe room for rent because I couldn't afford an apartment. I was very lucky to get an information about a man who had his own family and wanted to rent one room out of his three-bedroom apartment.

I met him and we agreed on the price, and he told me that the room was ready, I didn't need a bed or anything. Just my bag of clothes and shoes.

That was exactly what happened, I moved into the apartment room in Somerset.

After a few months, I got admission into a college to study Nursing. Yes, I needed something that would pay my bills and give me extra money.

School was tedious and I also worked at nights, I didn't have time for nonsense.

For Sam, I started dating him and we were cool with each other. He wanted me to go to Nigeria with him so we could meet his mother, he had no clue. And since that fake prayer woman told me that a man was waiting for me abroad, I decided to give it a trial.

I was busy with school, and church altogether. Weekend was for Church starting from Friday night prayers. Though I would still receive calls from Chris, I was just holding on to see what became of us.

During one of my classes in school, I met a Ghanaian girl who was always talking about her baby's father who was from Nigeria. One day we were assigned a project together in my Microbiology class, and she was a little late. She told me her baby father was supposed to pick her two-year-old son up so she could come to school early, but he was late.

And out of curiosity, I asked who was her baby father? She told me his name was Sam who was a computer guy and worked for IBM.

I lost my brain cells from hearing that name. I was frozen to the floor. And I was quiet for some time before telling her that I actually have a friend by that name and descriptions. She was a very loud girl and I was worried about Sam; how did he meet a girl like her.

I kept my calm; I was saddened to my soul. After class, once I got home, I called Sam because he had stopped by to see me before I went to class. And this girl lived up the street from me. I called him and I said to him that I know things happen in life, but he should have told me he had a two-year-old son. He didn't have to wait for me to find out the way I did.

That was the end of Sam. Oh no, he pleaded, he tried every means to convince me, but I was done. I told him I couldn't trust him anymore and didn't think it was ok pretending with him. I just focused in school and church. Anyway, this is just part of the story. I would return to the other part later.

When the pastor of the Nigerian Church saw how much I was dedicated to the things of God, he drew me closer to his family. His wife was a very gentle young woman and they had two kids then.

When he got to know more about me, that I had someone called Chris in Nigeria, he wanted to know Chris. He was a very controlling pastor and wanted to get involved in everyone's family matters, I came to know this later.

By late 2005, I was able to convince my daddy about Chris. My dad listens to my sister a lot and she had already poisoned his mind about me being in America and being married to a man in Nigeria. My daddy was concerned about the long-distance relationship.

He agreed with me about my choice and told me I can tell Chris to come home and bring his parents for a formal marriage introduction.

When my bride price (dowry) was paid, my sister didn't know about it. My parents just kept her out of it.

By 2006, the pastor being manipulative as he could be wanted to have personal information about Chris, he called me his daughter and I was close to his family.

But Chris wasn't going to fall for him; he is too stubborn to entertain any pastor. So, when pastor told me to tell him to call him, he wanted to find out his plans concerning coming to America.

Chris was so upset when I made that request that my pastor wanted him to call him. He yelled at me, he told me to tell him to mind his business because he is not my father and shouldn't try to be important.

The Pastor was upset about Chris ignoring him. What was I doing with myself? I was pushed around a lot all in the name of Church services.

During the Christmas of 2006, Chris wanted me home, now I was officially his wife. After exams, I had about three weeks break from school. Chris bought my ticket, and I was home. Yes, I was in Lagos, and very happy.

It was different once I saw Chris, it was so different. The long distance had so much pressure on our relationship. So, we agreed that every six months I would come home.

In December 27th, 2006, we got married at the Lagos high court. Then we flew to the East to see my parents.

You remember Sumbo from the Nigerian church back in the USA? She was in Lagos meeting her husband too, and I begged her to come with her husband to become a witness to our marriage in Lagos high court. It happened just the way we planned it. There were no family members involved because I just needed the official marriage documents to apply for Chris's visiting papers to the US. That was all, the Church wedding was scheduled for August 2007, since I was graduating from nursing school by May 2007.

Troubled Pastor

When I returned from Nigeria, the pastor saw all the wedding pictures. Not sure what happened to him, but he wasn't happy from the looks of things.

He started making silly comments about him, and how Chris's mother wanted me as a money-making machine. I told the pastor that Chris has his own business and was doing well in Lagos, there was no need for wanting my money. At least he is the one who gave me money, and not the other way around. The Pastor was jealous, he wasn't going to let anyone take me away from his church, I was a dedicated worker. I believe he wanted a guy he could manipulate and was so scared that when Chris comes into the US, he would take me away from his church. That was exactly Chris's plan for him. I was always saying my pastor said this, did that, he was so sick of him. Equally on the other hand, I guess somehow, pastor figured out that Chris was a strong character and was not malleable, so he did not want me with him. Nonetheless, neither me nor Chris anticipated what circumstances would unfold in our long-distance relationship and the next series of events opened up life changing experiences with huge ramifications for us and teachable moments for any individual who gets acquainted to this story.

Separation from Chris

After Chris paid my bride price, my perception of him changed. He appeared more problematic. He continued with his lifestyle and didn't listen to any contributions I had to make regarding the marriage plans.

He was under a spell, probably from the people who didn't want us married.

After we choose a date for the wedding, I had told my family and friends. Arranged for my bridesmaids etc. everything was happening so fast. Suddenly, he called me and told me he was calling the wedding off. He wanted to visit the US first, and we could figure out the date for the wedding. That plan was very fishy, and I didn't understand why he would call off a wedding, just to come to America first.

For the first time, I threatened him that if the wedding didn't hold in August as planned, I would take that as a sign that we were not meant to be together.

He was very stubborn and didn't listen to anything I was saying. He thought I loved him too much and was unable to let him go, he could prove that. But on the other hand, my sister was giving me hell, my brothers were divided on their support for my wedding and it tore me out.

I called my daddy and told him what Chris said and what I said to him. Daddy said we should take time and plan better; date shouldn't be a problem between us.

Chris was still calling me, and we would talk at length, but nothing about the wedding.

I told my pastor about my decisions and he was in support of it. He told me once that date was passed, I should change my phone number. That was exactly what I did. I ended the relationship. I was so sick of it especially without my sister's support and some of my brothers, she was already able to convince.

She insisted that my husband wasn't Chris and how God told her that my husband was actually in USA and not in Nigeria. That's how Chris got out of the picture. Well, it was all in the devil's plan. My sister never liked Chris. He was a man and too independent for her liking. My sister would neither control him nor me if we were married. That was just that and the circumstance worked to favor my sister's preconceived end.

The Challenges with My Pastor

Once I changed my phone number and Chris couldn't reach me any longer as planned, I called my parents and my brothers and told them what happened, and how I have decided to move on with my life. Some of them were totally in agreement with me, but those that my sister was working with were happy.

My sister became my best friend, she called quiet often just to encourage me. At least for a moment I had peace in everything.

I had plenty of suitors, but I couldn't move forward with them because my bride price was paid by Chris, and in other to move on to marry any other man, his paid price would have to be taken back to his home. And he would agree to take it back for me to be freed.

It was the tradition, a culture that has existed for ages. There are consequences for doing things wrong. On the other hand, Chris didn't want his paid price back. He told his father not to take it back.

You remember Queendaline? she married her heartthrob Jeff, and they both lived in the U.K. with their two kids. Though I changed my phone number, but some of my family members had my new number including my cousin Queendaline. And I had warned everyone about giving my number out to anyone.

I heard Chris was devastated through my cousin Queendaline, but I wasn't shaken. Even though personally I had a lot to deal with in the aftermath of the break, I had moved on just for peace to reign. Though, I wasn't particularly happy with what was going on with him, I was done with his pride and stubbornness, he was so full of himself.

My pastor on the other hand was pounding so hard, he wanted me to consider dating some people in his church. He would call me to his office after service and make jokes about certain brothers in the Church. Very annoying jokes, he didn't know me very well, he didn't know what I was capable of doing.

One day during his usual jokes, I snapped at him and I told him to stop. I didn't need to date anyone he was offering to me.

I told him that they were boys and not men. I told him the people he was offering to me to date wouldn't stand me. I told my pastor that shoes have sizes and they were not my size.

You know by now I was already a nurse and making money, so every poor thing wanted to hook up with me.

Fall out with My Pastor

There were plenty of people who visited the church, and they did notice me. I was the head usher now since Sumbo, the former head usher got married and moved on from the church. Her husband didn't want to have anything to do with my pastor either, he was overly controlling.

One woman of God visited, and I was the one who catered to her. In the process of working with her, I noticed her phone was shattered and she couldn't make any calls.

I had a brand-new Blackberry phone; I believe that was the phone everyone wanted at that time. It was just hot like the iPhone series. I was working as a nurse and I had some money to throw around. I gave the woman of God, prophetess as she was called my brand-new phone. I just took my SIM card out and gave her the phone. I had an old phone at home, and I could easily get another phone.

When the woman of God told my pastor what happened between us, he was enraged; the woman of God was only telling him just to thank me for the gift.

He called me when I got home and yelled at me over the phone, he told me if the woman wanted a phone, he could buy her one. He didn't give me any chance to explain to him what led to me giving her my brand-new phone.

I put the incidence on record for my pastor, he was becoming very obnoxious and annoying. At a point, he had my check book and my debit card, he had sold me the idea that he wanted me to buy a house and was forcing me to save my money.

Everything that was wrong about my relationship with the Pastor is that he wanted to know where I was and what I was doing, he wanted me to only spend time with his family. He was overly protective and monitored every move I made. I was the head usher, and also held the church account deposit keys. He put me in control of the offerings at church. After service I stayed back to count the money and would take the money to deposit at the bank the next day. Yes, he trusted me. Well, all my money was also being sown into the church. I would write $1000 check for church support now and then. That was how it worked.

How did he get me to this corner? When I moved out of first house I stayed, the car the lady gave to me, I had to return it. My pastor was the person who co-signed for me to get a car. I got a brand-new car afterwards. Nonetheless, because I had no credit history, I needed someone to co-sign my car note. My pastor offered to help me out. After he did that, I became indebted to him. He became like a father to me, and I laid down my guard. He was just too overbearing, I couldn't breathe.

He was so jealous, he didn't want anyone else around me, because he was afraid, they were going to take me away from his church.

The phone I gave to the woman of God, made an impression on her, and she vowed to be there for me somehow. She would call me to check on me, and I knew not to tell my pastor that she called me.

And one day, she called me and prayed for me over the phone. She asked me about marriage, I told her some of the things that had happened to me.

By this time, there was a friend, a colleague at work who liked me too much and wanted her brother in Europe to get to know me. I was becoming a little secretive about my way and I didn't tell my pastor anything more than what I wanted him to know. I wanted to be free from him.

So, I decided to go visit my cousin in the U.K. and I called up this my colleague's brother. Yeah, she gave me his number, and I said I was going to call him to come see me.

I called him, and he came to Queendaline's house to say hi. We got acquainted with each other, and he left. We started talking on the phone. He wanted marriage. Every man that came across me wanted me to be his wife, no one wanted me as a girlfriend.

When I returned home from that trip, I had made up my mind to move forward.

My pastor told me the church had a need, and God wanted me to buy a bus for the church in order to transport people who were having it challenging commuting to church.

That made me more upset and I decided I was going to ignore him. I literally just sowed a seed of $5000 towards the church's new building, and now he wants me to buy a bus for the church.

The woman of God, the prophetess called me and told me something that encouraged me to move forward.

She told me that another man of God called her and told her the things my pastor said about me, how I can't go anywhere unless he approves of it. What a manipulation! She told me to leave the church because if I stayed around my pastor, I would never get married.

Pregnancy

When I dated that guy called Sam, in the process of getting to know him better, after I moved out of the lady's house, I got pregnant. I had never been pregnant before, so I didn't know how it felt to be pregnant. I just noticed that I missed my monthly period which had never happened to me. I am one of those lucky women to experience regularity with their monthly cycles.

After I missed my period, I told Sam what happened to me. He told me it was ok, not to worry, that he would take me to a doctor on Monday morning. This was on a Saturday, and first thing Monday morning I was at his place. He drove me to this white doctor somewhere in Franklin Park. And when we got there, I thought we were going to just confirm if I was pregnant or not. When I got there, he checked me out, I did urine test; It was positive. Then the odd question, the doctor asked me if we were going to keep the pregnancy? He continued to say it's only five to six weeks based on his calculations. I was surprised to hear a thing like that, but looking at Sam, he outrightly said "no, not right now doctor …" I was still in shock. I had never been in such a situation before in my life. The doctor looked at me and saw my reaction, then he left the room for me and Sam to talk about what we were going to do about it.

Sam started by saying, "Chioma, you are literally in school, and I can't watch you suffer in this country. It is tough to carry pregnancy and a child while in school, we are not ready for any child right now"

I broke down, I cried my eyes out. First, I was scared to my marrow because I wasn't sure what this doctor planned to do to me. I said to Sam I was going to think about it, but he was so strong, and he said to me he thought about it throughout Saturday and Sunday, and he made up his mind that if I was pregnant, we were not going to keep it. I cried again, and again, but Sam was able to convince me to abort the pregnancy.

The doctor came and I signed the papers, and he promised me it was nothing. The last thing I remembered was that I was given an injection and asked to lay down on his office examining table. The table used for GYN exams. I don't remember anything else except that when I woke up, he gave me instructions and some antibiotics. He turned to Sam and told him no sex for six weeks. It was during this time that I met the girl in my class who told me she had a two-year-old son for Sam.

I couldn't be a normal person after I just terminated my own pregnancy. I wasn't in church, and I was hiding from everyone including myself. Then my pastor called me challenging me that something was so wrong about me, and I broke down, cried for some minutes until he told me to come over to his house. In confidence I told my pastor what just happened to me. He was furious, he was enraged. And he demanded for Sam's number which I didn't hold back. My pastor called him and told him off, he told him to stay away from me.

That made Sam very mad, but it didn't stop him from coming by to check on me to see how I was coping. It was during one of those days that he stopped by to check on me that he delayed from picking up his child, which made his baby Mama very mad. She was puffing and cursing in class, until I asked who her baby father was; it was Sam.

Meanwhile, my pastor while having a discussion with another man of God who was visiting his Church, told him the things I told him in confidence. Though my pastor helped me heal at that dark period, I couldn't have done it alone, everything happened fast and unexpectedly and for sure God intervened in my life. Additionally, when I began to process all that happened, I was overwhelmed with grief and the devil laid a heavy burden on me. Of course, the Devil of America Wanted Me.

After my pastor told the man of God the things about me. The man of God turned around and told the woman of God (the prophetess) who truly loves me, the same story. That was why the prophetess was persuaded to encourage me to move. She was upset that my pastor that I trusted so much could talk about me in this manner to another man of God.

I listened to the woman of God, and she told me to leave the church if I wanted to get married. And she also told me that while praying for me, God told her that I left my husband, the guy in Nigeria. She advised me about going to a church called Faith Fellowship, managed by an Italian pastor, a great man of faith. She told me I must avoid any Nigerian church because these pastors have turned young girls into maids in Nigerian churches. Talking about Nigerian Churches, pastored by Nigerian pastors in the US in this light is a truism. Young girls from good Christian homes who happen to leave their families behind in Nigeria just to come over to the US as a result of open opportunities to them and in the effort to be guided by Nigerian pastors who understand their culture have been victims of deceit and wrong advices from these pastors and the simple reason for these occurrences is because of these pastor's selfish gains.

Nonetheless and for me personally, if not for the challenges I had initially, the pastor could never had crossed my part, but God was still in charge even though the Devil Wants Me.

Faith Fellowship

What a God sent church; Faith fellowship was a place I found peace. It reminded me of the serenity I had during benedictions as a child. It was a place I reconnected with God, I blocked off a lot of people out of my life. I wanted to hear from God directly. I have heard from God before, and through all these years, it was as if God was so quiet on me.

In fact, I felt after I drank that water from the dirty kettle back in Nigeria, God was quiet on me. I struggled with so many things, I was known for midnight crying. That's when I told God my problems, but he was still very quiet.

Guess what? I moved on from my pastor. I was already back in school finishing up my BS, I told him I couldn't make it to church because I took Sunday shifts at work. I was attending school during the week.

But I lied to him, I had already started attending Faith fellowship on Sunday mornings, it reminded me of Dominion City in Nigeria, so I felt an inner peace.

The U.K. Guy

The U.K. Guy was very serious, and his sister was pounding on me here and there to marry her brother. He was good looking and just few years-older than me. So, we wanted to give it a shot. In the process of getting to know him, I told him everything that happened between me and Chris, a clean truth. He wanted me so it didn't matter. He just wanted to find a way to give Chris back his paid bride price, so he can go ahead and marry me.

Chris on the other hand said I am his wife and that he wasn't letting any man have me. Oh yes, I was in a strange place, he refused to take back the bride price.

The U.K. guy was so serious, he wanted his family to meet with mine in Nigeria to see what could be done. They arranged and visited my parents, and I was told my big brother, the law maker (He is a Justice of a high court), yelled at them that according to the custom I was still married to Chris. He told them to tell their son to speak with me, and that if I didn't want Chris anymore, we should be able to agree on how he would take back his paid bride price.

I wasn't ready to talk to Chris, who by now was already destroyed emotionally.

I got my citizenship in 2008, so I was traveling a lot. I was going to Nigeria and would pass through Lagos without seeing Chris. I didn't want to see him, am sure he would have made me change my mind, so I avoided the sights of him.

When he heard that I came to Nigeria, and moved around without calling him, he was more devastated.

He began seeking help, praying, I guess. You remember when I went to Nigeria in 2006 after he paid my bride price. I was also going to Church in Lagos. Dominion City had just came into Lagos. Oh, I was dying to hear the words and the teachings of Pastor David Ogbueli. Chris would drop me off at Church on a Sunday morning, then go to his friend's house to hang out. He wasn't broken, he had too much power and he had money to throw around, so it was destroying him. He felt he didn't need any church. On a good Sunday, he would attend Sunday mass and that was it. He didn't want what I had, and that was why I was so strong that I needed someone that would yield to God.

By the time I visited Nigeria few times without seeing him, he went back looking for help from God. He remembered the Church where he used to drop me off, and he decided to try to see if he could find Jesus there. He visited a few times, and he was blown away with the teachings of Pastor

David Ogbueli. The man David Ogbueli had a fresh word every time, I am sure he still does.

That's how Chris confessed Jesus as his Lord, and he began the process of getting to know Jesus.

Chris called my cousin Queendaline and told her to tell me he is a changed person; he is a born again and also speaks in tongues.

My cousin called me to give me the news. Oh, how we made jokes about him and his newfound faith. I told my cousin he was faking, and that it was very late though. I told my cousin to tell him I wished him well and that we will meet in heaven someday. I didn't believe him, and I also didn't want to go back there again.

The U.K. Guy & His Mom

One thing my mother taught me was total respect and I had enough stored up, but I cannot withstand insults and abuse. I had already had enough at this time.

On a Sunday morning while returning home from a night shift, I got a call from the U.K. guy's mother, his sisters would call me, and I had also spoken to his brothers. This time around, it was his mother. I was driving, but I picked up the phone because I knew it was an international call.

She started off yelling at me, she told me she heard from her son that I used to be a Catholic and now I claim to be a born again. She continued her rambling on how she doesn't want me to come into her family with some problems. She doesn't want a divided family as she claimed.

At this point, I was so shocked, and I interrupted her. I said to her that I just finished a night shift and driving back from work. And I said to her she had not spoken to me before and doesn't know what I sounded like on the phone. I told her she was being very offensive, and I didn't want her to continue speaking to me, I told her not to call my phone again and I hanged up the phone.

Apparently, her son told her that I was attending a faith-based church in

New Jersey and that I didn't want to go back to Catholic Church. I made it clear to him what my faith was and that I wasn't going back to the Catholic Church.

That was the only issue he had with me, he wanted to remain a Catholic and he wanted me to come with him.

The following morning, he called me, and he was saying his mother said I yelled at her on the phone and told her not to call my phone again.

I told him, to go ahead and marry his mother because I wasn't interested anymore. I didn't need a mother in-law that yells at people. I would do anything to avoid a mother in-law that would give me issues and that included staying away from him. Yeah, I just told him to stay with his mother that I wasn't interested anymore.

He wanted us to talk about it, he called me for one week, but I wasn't having it.

I literally had no patience for any guy at all, so I just didn't want any more relationships. I quitted on everyone. And I changed my phone number again. No U.K. guy, no Nigerian guy, no pastors, everyone give me some space!

CHAPTER SIX

Letters from the Devil

ONCE I GRADUATED FROM SCHOOL and was working as a nurse, I could afford to pay about $950 monthly rent. I moved from somerset to Edison, a very nice city, and it was pretty expensive. I lived alone and the apartment was close to a Military base, some level of security for me as a young woman.

And once I moved and was comfortable, I started getting mails from the underworld. The mail came in, had my name on it, but had no return address or where the mail came from. The letter was a seven-page letter, and also told me things about me that I didn't know.

The letter said that whoever was the writer (the devil) had monitored me since I entered the USA. It told me that the reason I entered the USA was because they were interested in me as a person. The letter was so detailed that I was shaking reading it, but I summoned courage to continue to read.

Then the offers: the letter said to me, since I was born to do this, I would be moved to California, and I would choose a top five mansion I would love to live in. I would have access to money and would be among the top wealthy people in the USA.

It said, I was born with something special that they needed. And they are trying to make it official by extending this offer to me. It made me many other offers that once I closed the letter, I forgot some of them.

The letter said if I would like to take the offer to call a number given to me on the next page.

That's where I stopped, I didn't turn to the final page, I took the seven-page letter and ripped it into pieces. That night, I prayed so hard as I was saying to the Devil, I don't want you nor your offers. That was the beginning of my nightmares with the devil, but I was very courageous, and I continued with my life

Although I knew I was being followed and monitored. After about one year, I got another dose of the same letter, with increased offers. And I just did the same thing after reading it.

By this time, my circumstance changed. I was targeted at work, the doctors picked on me, along with my nurse managers, including my colleagues at work.

Then I devised a means of surviving. Even though I was still attending the Nigerian church when I started getting these letters. I didn't tell anyone about it.

God would still say little words into my spirit like on one occasion, he told me remember the woman at the garden (Eden), it sounds like what the devil is trying to do with you.

That word strengthened me, and I braced myself for war.

I tried to digest some of the statements from that letter, and I didn't know if I should believe the letter or not. It said I was brought to USA for this mission, and that's why my green card didn't come in time, because I was here for a mission.

Now, I was asking myself what mission are they talking about? How did I get myself into this mission? All I could remember was how I gave my life to Jesus over and over. When did I get into anything with the devil, I asked myself?

But I also remember that the Devil is a chief deceiver and lies a lot. I continued about with my life. By the time I got the second letter, I had already left the Nigerian church and moved on with my life.

I was very busy with school because I decided after my BS in Nursing to go for my master and to also get a medical examiner's certification, at least to see if I can become an independent practitioner.

A Strange dream

Once I started attending Church services at Faith fellowship and tried to strengthen my faith in God, I started believing in the voice of God again.

By March 2010, just around about the Easter period, I had fasted and prayed to God for forgiveness and to please lead me in the right part concerning the area of marriage.

And one of my prayer points was to soften the heart of Chris so he could accept his paid bride price and we can both move on with our lives.

After I ended this prayer, I had a dream. In this dream I was taken to Chris's village and his house was covered with cobwebs, especially the entrance to the house.

While standing and watching what was happening, I saw his little sister walk out of the house, and I woke up.

Three days after the dream, I summoned the courage to call him, to plead with him to see if he could let me go. I sent him a text message to let him know I was the one and that I wanted to speak to him, remember he didn't have my new phone number.

And he asked if he could call me, and I said yes. He called me and he started off by saying "my beautiful, you are a blessed woman and I know that God is watching over you..." but I had to stop him. I told him that wasn't what I wanted to speak to him about. I wanted to plead with him to have mercy on me and just take back his paid bride price so we can both move on with our lives.

He told me that wasn't what God told him, he told me he just finished Camp meeting at Dominion City, the same camp meeting that I used to attend back in Nigeria and that he had also fasted for 40 days. He said, God promised to bring his wife back. I told him that God didn't say anything to me. And I told him that I would talk to him later and I hung up the phone.

I was confused, but I was quiet about it. I then remembered the woman of God who told me to leave the Nigerian church to Faith fellowship.

She had called me back in 2009 while I was traveling to U.K., and she told me that she didn't see my future with the U.K. guy, and she also told me that she sees me as married and that guy in Nigeria is the only guy that I have a future with.

I wasn't going to allow any of those anymore. The woman in Nigeria told me my husband was waiting for me in America, while this other woman of God is saying I left my husband in Nigeria.

Before then, I had called my sister and as I had played into her hands, she was helping me to pray over the situation. Additionally, even though I didn't tell my sister what the woman of God in the US had told me, I just wanted to know the outcome of her own prayer group. My sister had a prayer group that can overturn any situation, except I don't know the source of the power.

My sister then told me that they tried to break the bond between me and Chris; but couldn't. she told me the prayer people said it was so strong. And they had suggested that I had a blood covenant with Chris. Blood covenant I said? I told her that Chris was the first man I had sexual contact with, could that have contributed as a blood covenant? I am sure she was shocked to hear that at the age when I met Chris, I was still a virgin.

My sister and her husband used to accuse me of so many things, how men were after me, and how someone told them they saw me with a guy somewhere in a bar. I was always either cooking or cleaning or washing clothes at her house, I barely had time to breathe, and they still accused me of things that I couldn't imagine.

There was nothing I wasn't accused of; all I did was tell them I didn't do it and cried afterwards.

After speaking to Chris, I was confused again. The gross confusion led me to pouring out tears every night for another three days, because I wasn't sure what I would tell my family again and that was my circumstance. Then I heard a voice tell me one night, "you left your house in ruins" and I cried the more. I asked God to forgive me that I was sorry to be in this position. Nevertheless, that was my situation and of course, the Devil Wanted Me.

The next day Chris sent me a text message asking if he could call me, and I said yes. Immediately he called me, I couldn't control myself anymore, I was weeping and weeping, and I told him I was tired of life and everything.

Then, he asked if I would want to come home? Shockingly, I said yes, I wanted to come home.

I had just started my master's degree program and was going to get a break in May, then I could go home.

This was happening in April, so by End of May I was in Nigeria. I told my family I was coming home sometime in May, but I didn't tell them exactly when. I wanted to finish up whatever I was doing with Chris, then figure out how to tell them that I went back to Chris.

When I got home, I was so emotional, I could cry just by any means. After one week in Lagos with Chris, I traveled to see my brother Okechukwu in Abuja. He is my friendly brother, the one I could pour out my heart to without fears. I had told him everything, and he told me that if God was in it, He would work it out.

Then I traveled to see my sister who had no clue of what was happening. I just didn't let her know that I was back with Chris, a man who had paid my bride price four years ago. I just ignored her and let her live in her world of control and of course, I knew my sister would not support me.

When I traveled to see my parents, I told them the status and, that's where my heart was. My father said it was ok, that he has never seen the young man as a bad person, he just wants me to be happy. We all agreed to leave my sister out of it until later when we will be ready for the wedding. I was in Nigeria for six weeks then returned back to the USA.

First Child

Once I returned back to the US, I noticed changes in my body, and I had missed my period. I Did a pregnancy test and it was positive!

Chris was very happy, he wanted it to happen and it did. And now we had to rapidly plan for the wedding. By August I was in Nigeria again, though you couldn't tell that I was pregnant, but if you knew me, you could tell of the changes.

When I got to Lagos, and called my sister and told her I was in Lagos, she wanted to know where I was in Lagos, and I told her I was with Chris. She hung up the phone on me. I decided I wasn't going to call her again until I got down to the East.

I and Chris travelled together now to the East; we were making plans. Queendaline and Jeff her husband had relocated back to Nigeria after her husband finished his master's degree in the UK. So, she was able to help me with some of the preparations. We decided that everyone including Chris and her husband Jeff were going to visit my sister; to plead with her so she can allow the marriage to move forward. Imagine, my sister had to be begged and persuaded to let me marry Chris!

We got to her house and waited until she returned home from work. Chris and Jeff had to wait outside perhaps she may not want Chris in her house. To tell you the honest truth, I wondered for a long-time what Chris could have done to my sister. They never crossed parts and am not sure why she didn't want me to marry him. Now I know, I will save the gist for later.

After she returned home from work, while she ate, I and my cousin Queendaline told her what we wanted to talk to her about.

Immediately, she started yelling at both of us, and we got on our knees pleading with her to please forgive whatever wrong I might have done, and that I really love Chris and want to be with him. She continued to yell at me saying "Shame on you, look at you with pregnancy, shame on you " At this point I stopped her and I said to her, that traditionally I have been married to Chris, and my parents and uncles gave me out to him as a wife, where is the shame coming from? I said to her "you got married at the age of 20, and I am almost 29 without a child, and you call it shame?" And I told her that I wanted to carry her along and that the wedding was going to hold in December. She said to me that the marriage wasn't going to hold, and that she was going to make sure it didn't hold. I got up from where I was kneeling, and I walked out of her house with my cousin Queendaline. We met Chris and Jeff who were waiting to see when she would allow them to come into her house. It didn't happen, and we got into the car and drove back to Abakaliki where I was staying with Chris.

A call came that night from my sister's husband, he continued from where his wife stopped, with abusive words. He said to me, what happened to you, are you a dog that you could go back to your vomit? How could you do such a thing. I stopped him, I said to him, that Chris is my husband, we just had a little issue like in any other marriage. And he said to me that he never knew I could go back to him. And I asked him, what exactly was wrong with Chris? He had no answer, and I was not surprised.

I know, it was all part of the plan, I wasn't supposed to marry anyone else. It had already been programmed to happen the way they wanted it, and I am rebelling. I am messing with them, and their kingdom. How dare you try to rebel? Of course, the Devil Wanted Me.

Part of it was that I was already programmed to marry a certain man in the USA, an occultist, perhaps an Illuminati member. From there, we could get to the next program. The devil of America really wants me, and he is so desperate.

CHAPTER SEVEN

T HE WEDDING PLANS MOVED ON and when I returned back to USA, I had to continue making the plans. You remember back in 2007, when suddenly Chris changed his mind about the wedding date? I had already bought everything we needed for the wedding. My wedding dress, the bridesmaid, the groom and his best man. Everything was ready before that sudden change. He gave me money back in 2007 for the rings and I fitted mine and his was just fine.

Thank God for that, I didn't have to pay for anything else except to refit my custom designed wedding dress due to pregnancy. Chris had money and I was already working as a nurse, so while he paid for the diamond rings, I paid for the clothes. We were set to go, except that my brothers were calling me and telling me to try to work with my sister. They argued with me that she is my only sister and that she needs to be at my wedding.

Anyway, I called her, and requested if there was anything, she could help me do for the wedding?

And she volunteered to find someone to cater for the food. I was worried, she said they have people who catered at her prayer group in church, and she would have them make the wedding food.

Oh no! She wasn't going to pay for it, we were going to pay for it. After choosing the menu to be served at the wedding, she told me it was going to cost us #250000. Two hundred and fifty thousand Naira. That was too much for a local caterer. I had my friend Chinwe in Maryland, USA who was going to have her friend who was a caterer do it for One hundred and fifty thousand. Chris on the hand was fuming that the money was too much. But I told him to just let her have her way because I didn't want any further issues from her.

The Wedding

Two days before the wedding, I got a call from my sister that we needed to give her extra money because things were expensive at the market. She requested an extra #50000 (fifty thousand Naira). It wasn't happening, Chris told me, we spent almost everything we had in reserve and we couldn't afford to give her extra money. We told her that we would rather get a different caterer. Yes, we called a caterer called "Madam Guess" who was actually going to take #200000 two hundred thousand Naira because the catering contract was at a short notice. I got back to my sister and told her not to bother about the catering anymore, that I would take the money back. What I planned to do was pay the other woman to make the food and forget about her. I still had some money on me, I was very prepared to face anything.

But my big brother Patty, got involved, and pleaded with her to stop her troubles. You remember how she had said, she wasn't going to let the marriage happen! I wasn't sure if that was what she planned to do.

I had wonderful friends who came together to make sure it happened. My course mate back in UNEC Maryjane (MJ Madu) stepped in and arranged for the colorful ladies of the day.

And my sisterly friend madam Chinedu Ozomgbachi, organized and paid for weddings souvenirs; God was so good to us. My friend, Chinwe Okudo, paid for the cake, I have good friends.

Guess what! My sister didn't attend the church wedding. She had an excuse that the hall was not in order, and she needed to help arrange for things. Someone was paid to take care of that and this lady actually got to the hall by 6 am in the morning with her entire group of decorators. I didn't make a big deal out of it; I just was heavily pregnant to continue with issues that weren't going to change anything. It was a wonderful wedding and we were happily ever after.

On our way back to Lagos, we stopped at her house in Enugu just to thank her for her wonderful support, and that was the end of the physical phase.

CHAPTER EIGHT

The dreams and encounters

A FTER I HAD THE BABY, I filed for Chris's green card. Though it took a little while, before the baby was one year plus, Chris had joined us.

After the wedding, my relationship with my sister was back to normal. We were close again. I told her everything that happened to me, what I did and didn't do. I also told her everything about Chris. When Chris came, I thought it was going to be a breeze for him to get a job. I mean he is a computer engineer with all these experiences, but it didn't happen the way I had expected.

Life was a bit challenging, I had completed my masters and sat for my certification exam for the advanced family nursing practice. I got a better job, we were not struggling financially, but I didn't want my husband at home, it was irritating.

So, I called my sister to help me pray as usual; everything to me is always prayer. If something was wrong, I would pray about it. Though I never consulted anyone to pray for me except my sister, I wanted to have a relationship with her by all means. I admired her as a young child, and I wanted to relate well with her, but she was so different, with a personality totally different from my mother.

On one of the occasions where I was telling her about my marriage, I told her I had a fight with Chris because he was looking to go back to school rather than sit at home to continue looking for a job. I would never forget what she told me. She told me to send him out of the house. I was shocked to my bones, my sister told me to send my husband out of the house. Anyway, I was naïve. I erroneously thought my sister was with me.

When I returned home, I was so worried about what my own sister advised me to do to my husband. And while praying that night, when I asked God to please help my husband get a job, I heard the voice of God very clearly that night. He said, if you want your marriage to work, stop talking to your sister about your husband. And the Holy Spirit became my best friend as always. I started communicating to the Holy Spirit and things picked up.

My sister called me every couple of days, and I told her things were alright; I had to cut her off before she ruined my marriage. There were no major discussion between us anymore except about my brothers and their wives. I took my relationship and marriage out of anyone's hands.

The third letter from the devil: the Devil wrote for the last time

After about the fourth month that Chris joined me and the baby, mind you I had already moved for the third time. To a better place, close to the metropolitan rail station where you can easily hop on the train and you will find yourself in New York City. Normally, I used to walk down to the metro park station and just hop on a train, and I will end up at the Times Square, New York. I was very happy for this place; it was for people who worked in NYC, so it was even more expensive. I was an emergency room trauma nurse when I moved to this apartment. I was paid well and the money to pay a monthly rent well over a thousand dollars wasn't an issue.

Nonetheless, the third letter came and had the same content, with a little twist to it. The letter said in the whole world, there were only five people who were like me and in the letter, I was made all the previous offers again.

This time around the circumstance was different. I told Chris about the other two letters in the past. For mention, I got the second letter in 2009, exactly three years from then.

He told me in confidence that I wouldn't get such letters anymore. He took his Bible and prayed over the letter and lit it on fire outside. He watched the letters burn. Oh my! That was the last time I got letters from the devil. But the Devil wasn't done with me, he became very mad at me, and the battle started.

After Chris joined us in 2012, we tried to have another baby, but it didn't happen. And I didn't really bother because my first son was only one year and few months.

By the following year, I started having nightmares and strange dreams. I know that God speaks to me, and I try to deepen my relationship with God. And being that Chris could pray now, things were a little better, though we still had struggles and few challenges.

First dream

One night, I was in a dream where my sister and her husband traveled to see a man. While they were visiting this strange one, I noticed they had the picture that I gave to her after my wedding. I had given her some of the wedding pictures to keep. And I saw her take this picture with her husband, and they told this man they didn't want me to have any more children. And immediately she said that, I awoke out of that dream sweating.

I was like nah! That's a crazy dream, my sister couldn't do a thing like that. I said someone wants me to hate my sister, someone is impersonating her, using her face to attack me in the dream.

Then, I remembered another dream that I had while I was pregnant with my first son. After I returned back from Nigeria before the trip for the wedding, I had a dream where someone entered my room in the middle of the night, and forcefully put the whole hand into my canal and tried to pull the baby out of my womb, and when I saw this person, I shouted, and this person had his right hand full of blood. I woke up sweating and I rushed to the bathroom. I thought I was having a miscarriage, but there was no blood physically. Thank God for a praying husband, I called him at 4 am that morning and he assured me to go back to sleep that it wasn't going to happen again, and it didn't until I had the baby.

So, when this second dream came, I had a flash back of the other dream. But I told myself it wasn't going to happen. My mother had 10 children, and my sister had six children, why would I end up with just one child. I prayed again, and boom I was pregnant by 2013.

Another Dream

After few weeks, I had another dream; in this dream, I was taken to somewhere in Nigeria, and I was in front of a house with a see-through curtain, without a door. It was as if someone called me and said follow me, I want to show you something.

While standing there, suddenly I saw the lady that I used to stay at her house. You remember the lady who played the visa lottery for everyone? I saw her in this dream. She had my picture with her and as she entered the house with the see-through curtain, I entered with her, she couldn't see me, but I could see her.

Inside this house was a man wearing tattered clothes, a short pant and ripped shirt. This man could see me, but she still couldn't see me. She started a conversation with this man, while she was talking, the man said to me, "what are you doing here? I didn't call you here" I turned and walked out of the room. But I stood by the entrance and I was eavesdropping on what they were saying.

She handed my picture to this man, she said to him, I want you to finish her up! And the man looked at me, and the conversation continued. He said to her, "why do you want to finish her up? You have done so much to her, and she hasn't done anything to you in return.

He said to her, God is angry with you, and your cup is full. The only way you can escape God's judgement is to call her and tell her what you have been doing against her and beg her for forgiveness.

And he said to her, she has a forgiving heart and will forgive you, but you need to call and tell her the things you have done against her"

As she made her way towards the curtain, I walked away, and I awoke out of that dream.

Again, I was so confused about this dream. I said again, no way will this person try to hurt me.

We literally talk every week, and whenever she calls me, she wants to know how we are doing?

I was telling her everything about me. I was just naïve. We used to be very close. You know when I got to her house; the first day I entered the US, we talked until about 2 AM in the morning. And while I was at her house, we used to watch midnight movies together, including X rated movies. We talked about so many intimate things, how could she try to hurt me? What did I do wrong? Even after I moved out of her house, I still visited her some weekend, sometimes to help her cook, especially whenever she was expecting visitors.

If she had somewhere to go with her husband, I would be at her house babysitting her son. Additionally, she used to call me up to help her make some jollof rice when she had a party or expecting some special guests. How on earth would a person like this want to hurt me?

I took that dream and placed it somewhere. Out of precaution I just didn't tell her many things about myself any longer. I used to tell her details about my work, how I was treated at work, my husband and where he worked and other things. I decided to slow down on things.

The third dream

I was six weeks pregnant with my second child. One afternoon as I was sleeping on the couch, I suddenly had a dream; someone walked into my house and tried to choke me while I was on this couch. Suddenly, a man appeared beside me and hit the person that was trying to choke me, though I couldn't see the face of this person who was trying to choke me, but I was aware of what just happened. Furthermore, the one who defended me, told me what the baby's name should be called and vanished.

I woke up sweating and my husband was at the dining table. I asked him if he saw the man who tried to choke me and the one who stopped him, and he said no.

By this time, I had enough, and I decided I was going to do something about these dreams.

I called my sister to try to get her prayer group to start praying for me. She told me it would be better if I returned home to attend some serious prayers. I told her about my last two dreams, except the first one she was involved. And we agreed that all the troubles were becoming too much. Since it was November, I would work towards returning home for Christmas, then attend the end of the year prayer with Adoration ministry at Enugu.

Although, the dreams continued, I was already heading for a solution which was the prayer retreat.

I discussed with my husband and he agreed with me to go. He said I needed rest since I was starting a new Job in January. I was being credentialed for a Family care practice job that I had just got. It was a big transition. It was going to pay me almost double of my nursing salary.

I was excited, but I needed to pray to get me ready for the new career adventure.

I landed in Nigeria safely and was in my sister's house for three whole weeks. I told her, I didn't want to travel back and forth to the village, and since I was going to be in Nigeria for five weeks, I will take time to go home to see my parents and my parents' in-laws before returning back to the USA. I wasn't joking when I told her I came home to pray.

Celine my dearest friend

Celine was a very close friend when I lived with my sister. We attended the same religious group within the Catholic Church, which made us become like sisters.

Celine attended a boarding school, so I only got to see her whenever school was closed and that was until we were out of High school. Anyway, as I landed in Nigeria that December, I went to her house to surprise her. She was so excited to see me and we spent the three weeks together.

I told her about the bad dreams, and she told me about a man of God who helped her out when she was going through a similar situation. She married a man whose father was an occultist, and had experienced hell.

She volunteered to take me to this man of God, Prophet Chike. I didn't tell my sister about it because, she was always antagonistic of any man of God who is not a Catholic.

When we got to prophet Chike, he looked at me few times and he told me to sit down that I was pregnant. My friend didn't know I was pregnant, I didn't tell her nor my sister. I made up my mind I wasn't going to tell anyone certain things about me. The pregnancy was just about two months plus, and I was a little skinny. You couldn't really tell that I was pregnant.

Once he told me that I was pregnant, he asked me if I knew the sex of the baby I said yes. And I told him about my dreams and how a man told me what the name was going to be.

Prophet Chike told me things about me that I didn't know; he looked at me again and said to me "look at you, do you know who you are? you don't know who you are"

He started by telling me that the Devil Really Wants me, and also, he told me never to step into any celestial prayer house or anywhere that spiritualists use celestial powers. I didn't really understand. I just wanted solutions for my bad dreams.

He told me many things but, out of the many things he told me, one was resounding to me.

He said "What You Carry is a kind of thing that if you ever allow the devil to use you; the Devil would use you against men with great destinies"

He said, every man I slept with would have to die after five years if I let the devil have me. He equally said that I would be so rich and very influential in the whole world. He said to me "that is why they are after you, because you refused to be used by the Devil"

I was baffled and I then remembered the letters I received from the Devil. I didn't tell anyone about these letters and their contents except for my husband.

Now, I was more open to hearing and being prayed for by this prophet of God. His solution was to get to my father's land in the village and pray over there.

We arranged for that and after the seven days prayer and fasting he gave me to complete, we traveled together to the village. We prayed there with everyone and I returned back to my sister's house. I didn't tell my sister I was going with anyone, I just told her I was going to the village to see my people.

After the prayers from the prophet, I was so relieved. I realized what I was up against. As the Devil was saying what he was saying on those letters, he wasn't joking about what his mission for me was, the Devil Really Wants Me.

CHAPTER NINE

Meeting the Adoration Priest

M Y SISTER WAS THE HEAD of the women's group at the Adoration Ministry in Enugu.

The priest was very busy, and you could hardly be lucky to see him, but because of all the things I told my sister that I had experienced, she offered to get me to see him.

Even though I didn't really care anymore after I met prophet Chike, I believed that I was in a good position. I had given prophet Chike my number and we were communicating pretty much every day. Nonetheless, I didn't want my sister to feel slighted, I agreed to meet with the priest.

There is usually a special service on New Year's day where the priest travels to his family house in his community, to celebrate his first Mass for the year. He usually does this to bless them and get them prepared for the year.

My sister being the head of the women's group was expected to be in attendance and she wanted me to come with her. When we got to the parish house at the church where the priest lived, my sister offered that I should join him in his own car with few other people. My sister had few other women in her own car, and since the priest had a Toyota 4 Runner, she said I would be more comfortable in his car because of the bumpy road.

While riding in his car, he kept staring at me via the rare view mirror, though we were talking, he stared at me again and he said to me, "I hope you will be as influential as your sister?' I wasn't sure what he meant, but

I told him my sister and I are two different individuals, and I wouldn't want to be anyone else. I want to be me. He understood I wasn't in the mood for it. Maybe the pregnancy hormones, I couldn't tell, but I was upset at that question.

We completed that service, and I told my sister that I would be riding back with her, not the priest. I didn't want to snap at him. There were things I noticed that I didn't quite agree with.

Holy Mass

Within that week, one faithful evening, my sister drove me to the priest's residence. In his residence, he had a chapel on the last floor, more like an upper room kind of setting. There were no chairs, and everyone who came in there either sat on the floor or stood.

You didn't wear shoes to the chapel, you would come in bare footed and be on the floor.

While we were waiting in his visitors' room downstairs, two men and the priest walked in, greeted us, and went upstairs to the chapel. After few minutes my sister told me we have to go up to meet them.

When we got into the chapel, the priest started his mass, he was going to celebrate mass before praying for me.

I wasn't disturbed, I used to be a Catholic, and mass celebration in the Eucharist was one of the greatest things that happened to anyone in the Catholic Church.

I noticed something abnormal during the homily, he stopped few times to ring a bell that he had on the altar. I grew up a Catholic and I had never seen a Catholic priest ringing bells in the middle of homily like the white garment churches. He did these three times then stopped.

During communion, he gave me bunch of them, and he told me to finish them, which I did. And I also noticed something else, after he drank the communion wine from the cup, he gave to the men who he brought with him, and then to my sister before giving to me. Like I said, I didn't want to be disrespectful, but I didn't think it was appropriate to share a cup of communion wine with strangers; the three men. I was a bit uncomfortable, but I just went with the flow.

After the communion, he ended the mass. While I was waiting for him to pray for me the way I was used to, by the laying of hands, it didn't happen. And I turned to my sister, and asked her if he was going to pray for me? My sister asked him that I was requesting. He told me that the mass he celebrated was best of any kind of prayer. I took it in good faith, and we left.

When I slept that night, I remembered I had dreams about being somewhere, but I woke up forgetting the dreams.

Queendaline's friend

When I eventually had enough of the three weeks in my sister's house, I traveled to Abakaliki to see my parents, along with Queendaline and other family members.

Queendaline had a friend who just received fresh fire from God and had a revelational gift. When she visited Queendaline, she met me at her house, while we were talking, she told me that there was a lady back in the USA who followed me about. She said she could see the lady telling some people in her secret place that she could get me anywhere she wanted. She continued to say, that this lady had been trying to get me initiated into whatever she belonged to, but they are wondering why I have proven so stubborn. She said this lady vowed on the life of her son that she would get me into her occultic society.

Now, I didn't tell Queendaline about the dream I had with someone trying to hurt me, but she said they were monitoring my husband and want him out of my life because he is very prayerful. Whoa! I said, and I thanked her for the words.

When I returned back to my sister's house, she wanted to know what Queendaline's friend told me when I mentioned I met her. Earlier on, she had warned me about Queen's friend. She told me not to listen to whatever the girl had to say because she wasn't genuine. So, when she asked me what the girl said, I just told her that she told me that some people were trying to hurt me in the USA.

When I returned back to the US, Queendaline's friend had asked her to find out if she could speak with me? and I gave her a call. She told me she didn't know how to tell me what she saw about my sister, because she could see my love towards my sister.

She told me that my sister pretends to be a prayerful person, but she is not. She said my sister belongs to some underground society, but she deceives people with her prayer routine.

She also told me that in this place where my sister belonged, (she didn't really give me a name of the place), they had warned her to leave me alone, that I am of a different spirit, and she would be sorry if she didn't. She said that my sister is very stubborn and doesn't let go.

She said the reason she didn't tell me when I was in Nigeria was because she didn't want me to get her in trouble with my sister. I told her not to worry that I had gathered my facts and she didn't have to worry about me telling her anything.

My relationship with my sister didn't change as much, I was just in denial. I just didn't tell her personal things about me anymore.

When it was time to leave my sister's house, I told her to buy me angel Michael's candle that I heard it drives away evil spirits. Using the candles was supposedly meant to remove devils from one's home if you light them at night. The candle was a big and was supposed to last for over two weeks. Nonetheless, the candle gave me more nightmares and after a few times of burning it, I thrashed it. Chris was furious to see me bring a candle from Nigeria to remove devils. Look, I was desperate and though I could pray, the battles at nights were becoming too much for me.

My sister's visit to USA

After I returned from Nigeria in February, my sister called me that she would be visiting with her husband to attend her son's graduation ceremony. Before she told me about her coming, I had a dream multiple times, where she had visited and stayed in my house, and when she was leaving, Chris packed his luggage and followed her home.

That was a funny dream, but I wasn't downplaying my dreams anymore. I was open to what God wanted to reveal to me, and I prayed to God that I wouldn't doubt anything He reveals to me anymore.

When it was getting closer to her coming in May, I had this same dream two more times.

I called a sister I met when I attended the Nigerian church. I told her my dreams about someone who visited my house and at the end of the visit, my husband packed up his luggage and left with her.

The sister asked me if someone was planning to visit me? And I said yes, my sister. She said you can't allow her to step into your home, she is after your marriage. And once she steps into your home, your marriage will be over.

She told me to thank God that I called her, because it was the exact same thing that happened to her. Someone visited her from Nigeria, by the end of the visit, her husband packed his bags and left her house.

I said to her, how can I not allow my only sister to step into my house when she visits the USA? She told me I could choose between staying with my only sister and staying married. That was strong, but it gave me the answer I needed to put up with the fight.

When she visited, she stayed in an extended stay location very close to the city. I had made the arrangements so as to give them access to major cities and shopping malls. I made sure she was comfortable. She had brand new cooking utensils, and I had also made different kinds of food that will last them for a few days before they could decide what they wanted.

I made sure she was comfortable, and after work, I would stop by at her hotel to take them (she was with her husband and her last two kids) out for dinner and shopping.

The days that Chris was off from work, he visited them to take my brother-in-law (my sister's husband) shopping. He shopped differently. So, we were rotating the visits. And sometimes we would both end up with them at the hotel and stay with them until midnight.

They were happy and we were happy to make them comfortable.

Few times, my sister insisted she wanted me to pick them up so she could visit my house. I told her I was going to do that over the weekend. Though I didn't tell Chris this particular dream, I made him aware that I didn't want my sister visiting the house. He was shocked, but just left it alone. He had suggested to pick them up, and have them spend time with him at home even though I was at work, I said no.

I took some time off from work, and we took them to the liberty state park and took the ferry to New York, visiting the lady liberty statue, we made their stay a little fun.

Finally, the weekend came, and she wanted to go shopping. I picked her up with her friend who was also visiting for her own son's graduation. Both of them had been friends for ages.

We spent the whole day shopping, she loves to shop, and she was prepared to do it. By the time we got to their husbands at the hotel I was tired. I was about eight months pregnant at this point. I just told her I would see about tomorrow which was the only day they had before their departure first thing Monday morning.

That night, she called me that her husband's niece, the one I stayed at her house when I got to the US was having a get together for them tomorrow being Sunday. She had invited her important friends and my sister wanted me to come to the party, but I was going nowhere because I was too exhausted from running around. I was very grateful to God for working out things this way.

What excuse on the earth could I have given her that will make her not come to my house that Sunday evening? If I couldn't pick her up because of pregnancy, she would ask that my husband picked them up.

Monday morning, they were ready to get to the airport which was eleven minutes away from them. We bid them goodbye, and they were gone. That was some kind of a trip!

CHAPTER TEN

Giving Birth

A FTER MY SISTER AND HER friend left the USA, my real nightmares started. But I was ready, I realized that God was in the battles that I was fighting, I had peace and more assurance of him taking me through it.

Another dream came to me, and in this one, my sister's friend with whom she visited the US, came at me and invited me to a church service. In this church service, the priest that my sister and I had visited in Nigeria was supposed to be the officiating priest. Being my kind of person, I agreed to come with her. And she led me into an old house where we lived with our parents growing up. In this old house, pregnant woman were coming to pick up their babies. Once I got in there, I saw all the women, and I didn't see any priest celebrating the mass. I turned to leave. I told this woman who brought me there, that I wasn't in need for any babies, that I have my own.

She tried to stop me from leaving, I pushed her away and ran out of that place. While I was out of the building, I saw a masquerade chasing me. This masquerade had a dead baby dangling on his neck with a rope. The masquerade wanted me to take the dead baby, but I said no that I didn't want a dead baby. The masquerade pursued me harder, and suddenly I heard a voice tell me to stop and pursue after the masquerade. So, I stopped, and with all the anger in me, I went after the masquerade who suddenly stopped, in shock the masquerade started to run away from me. Once I got to this masquerade, I grabbed the arm and wanted to break the arm off the body, and the masquerade yelled out for help. It was the voice of my sister yelling, pleading with me not to break her arm. I was taken aback, and I said to her "sister! Is it you trying to give me a dead baby?" then I awoke out of this dream. I was heavily pregnant and was sweating so hard. When my husband asked what was going on, I told him that my sister tried to give me a dead baby in the dream.

After this dream, I didn't pick up her phone calls anymore. And I told Chris not to pick her calls, until after delivery, we agreed not to speak to anyone from Nigeria.

After one week, I had another dream where I was wheeled into the theater for an operation. In this dream, the baby came out, but the placenta was stock in me. When they wheeled me in, I saw them taking my body away from the operating room to the mortuary.

This time around when I woke up, I gave up a cry to God. I became very emotional about this dream. I asked God some deep questions about my existence on the earth and if this was how he planned to take my life? To die giving birth to my baby. I was angry for the first time, and in ignorance, my anger was towards God. This is quite funny. I thought, why would God allow whoever it is, that wants me dead to really kill me?

It was in the obvious that I was still in denial, I didn't believe my sister would ever do anything to hurt me. I didn't know who could know her so well to use her against me in my dreams. Those were my thoughts at times.

One week before my due date, I had another dream. You remember her friend who invited me to the church service where they wanted to give me a dead baby? The same one who visited USA with her? She entered my dream again, then told me that my sister wanted her to take me somewhere. I asked her about this place, she told me not to worry that I will be fine.

I followed her into this place, which had a house standing in the middle of the Bush.

She told me to follow her and she led me into the house. She opened the door and held it for me to get in, then once I walked in, she slammed the door shut. The house was very dark, and I couldn't see anything. Suddenly, there was a light penetrating through the other end of the house in front of me. And I heard a voice which told me to follow that light. I followed the light, and once I got to the door, I heard the voice again telling me to push through the door, which I did. Once I pushed through the door, I was out of the house. As I was running out of this bush, I turned to look at the house once again, and I saw what was written on it, it said mortuary. And I awoke out of this dream. This time, I didn't cry, because I said whatever it was that they had planned for me, God got me out of it. God said no, I cannot die giving birth to my baby.

My OBGYN

My doctor suddenly called me that she would like to have me scheduled for a cesarean birth. I told her that we talked about it and I told her I didn't want a cesarean birth. She talked about my age and high risk, this and that, but I wasn't going into any operating room. Now I really became scared due to the dreams I had.

The pregnancy was forty weeks now, and the labor was not started yet. And because I had cesarean during my first pregnancy at 37 weeks. Yes, once I returned from Nigeria from my wedding ceremony, I was induced by this male doctor because the water around the baby was low. I ended up with a cesarean birth.

That was why I found a female doctor and told her the reason I came to her was because of my first experience. I had a very painful recovery after the cesarean; I didn't want that pain again.

Her argument was that since it was forty weeks and labor hadn't progressed, I wasn't eligible for Pitocin induction due to risk for rupture of the womb.

Chris prayed his life out, I could see the fear in his eyes, but he was so strong for me.

Edison Police

After the conversation with my doctor, I didn't pick up her phone calls anymore.

She called the police to tell them to check on me to make sure I was ok.

When the police rang the doorbell, I thought they were at the wrong door. Nope, they were looking for me. They told me that my doctor was at the hospital waiting for me and I haven't showed up, and for two days I haven't picked up her calls.

I Promised them that I would go to the hospital to get checked out. The next morning, I went to the hospital. My doctor saw me and had pity on me and tried to encourage me. I wasn't eating anymore because I had lost my appetite, but I am sure I wasn't going to die giving birth to a baby. I wasn't sure how the baby was going to come, but somehow, the baby was going to come out.

After the first 24 hours of being monitored, the labor progressed, and I was four centimeters dilated. I was happy, my husband was relieved a little. Then my doctor asked the nurse to give me just a little Pitocin to see if it can hasten things up. I was in pain, but I wasn't really bothered. After an hour the nurse checked again, and she said the cervix retracted back and was closed. They stopped the Pitocin and gave me some intravenous infusion to keep me hydrated.

The cervix opened a bit and closing again, happening a few more times. By now I had already been in the hospital for three days. I was tired, but I wasn't going to die giving birth to any of my babies.

Suddenly, the baby's heart beats started to drop, and my doctor began to yell at me. She said, "I am not going to deliver a vegetable as a baby" and once she said that, I ordered her out of my room. And I requested for the house doctor, an OBGYN, who was a very wonderful, and compassionate woman from the Middle East. She promised me a safe delivery, and she said she had watched everything that happened to me. I asked her if she could do the cesarean to get the baby out? She told me if I have confidence in her, then let's go for it. She had over twenty years of experience as an OBGYN. That was not the reason, I just trusted her more than my private doctor. I wasn't sure if my private doctor was sent to kill me. That was my thought, immediately she started talking about cesarean. I was very paranoid about her.

The house doctor called the OR (operating room), they prepared the operating room, called the anesthesiologist who prepared me. She was very smooth, I watched her take the baby out because I had epidural block; I didn't want them to put me to sleep. Within one hour, everything was done, and Chris could breathe again. After two days, I was discharged from the hospital, because I recovered quickly.

When I called my sister to tell her I had the baby, she was very excited. Her husband called to congratulate me.

After a few days, I got a call from my sister. I started picking up her calls again, after all, I didn't die giving birth. When I picked up the call, she asked me a very strange question, "how did you deliver the baby, was it by cesarean or natural birth?" I was so angry at her for asking that question. And I asked her why she would call me to find out how I delivered my baby? She said it didn't matter even if it was by cesarean at least the baby is healthy. I hung up on her and started my thinking. I have been trying to process all these events for years. And now, they have been processed.

Though I continued to relate with my sister, I was super careful. On one occasion, when my mother told me that my sister was complaining that I didn't pick up her calls anymore and her husband had the same complaint about me. I had to open up to my mother. I told my mother everything that had been happening to me, and how my sister participated in those things.

My mother confronted her, but she said someone must have been using her face or images to appear to me.

But I said to my mother, how is it that all these things are happening to me and connected to her own face. How is it that my mother's face hasn't been used for all these things?

How is it that out of all my family members, her face was singled out by whoever she claimed was behind the dreams? I told my mom that as she demonstrates praying so much, no one should be able to continuously use her image against me.

CHAPTER ELEVEN

Seeking solutions

WHILE THE PROBLEMS AND STRANGE encounters continued, life was becoming normal for me. I didn't know what to expect at nights, but I had faith and trust in God that he will not give my life into the hands of the wicked. I have come to know a bit more about the faithfulness of God, and His loving kindness.

One thanksgiving evening, we had visited a family friend Charles and Stella Igwebuike. While we had thanksgiving dinner, we were having conversations about churches and pastors. And suddenly Charles said to me, have you seen the South African pastor Alph Lukau? I said nope! and he went on and on about what a great man of God he is. Though I wasn't really interested, but that day after I got home, his name got stuck in my head. I decided to search him on YouTube. I found him and I started watching him from then.

Travel to South Africa

The issues I was having continued, and as a matter of fact, I began to see the priest that my sister took me to his residence in my sleep. I began to also see myself in different places, and sometimes it could be a gathering, with my sister and her friends in attendance. I understood what that meant, I decided to go deeper in prayer. Chris my husband is also very prayerful, he intensified his prayers.

By now, I had stopped picking up my sister's phone calls, and also stopped every communication with the other lady that I lived in her house on arrival into the US.

My dreams and encounters with the priest of the Adoration Ministry Enugu intensified, I wasn't sure what I got myself into by visiting his residence. One night, I was in a dream where he called me into a house with group of women, and while he was addressing us, he turned to me and he said authoritatively, " this place you entered is different, and I am just warning you so you know. In this place, you are not allowed to sleep with any man" while he was still speaking, I interrupted him, and I said excuse me father! as he is normally called. And I said, please where is this place that I entered? don't you know that I am a married woman, and of a child-bearing age? If I don't sleep with my husband, how can I have kids? And once I asked him those questions, I awoke from the dream.

I told Chris about this dream and I told him I really need a deliverance. I need a stronger man of God to pray for me. And since we had been watching Alph Lukau together, we agreed that I should attend one of his upcoming church-program specially organized for international visitors.

Meeting Alph Lukau

It was during the international visitor's program (IVP) that I decided to travel to South Africa. This program gives you an opportunity to meet pastor Alph Lukau and get him to lay hands on you.

All I wanted was a strong man of God like him to lay hands on me, that was my faith. Even though I was expecting that he would give me some answers to my dreams and encounters, I made up my mind that, even if that didn't happen, I just wanted him to lay hands on my head.

The program was packed, and he was very busy that Friday night. But something happened to me, while I was in the hotel room, I had a dream and in this dream, I saw the lady that I lived in her house in the USA, and we both had a long discussion; though when I woke up from this dream, I forgot what the discussion was about.

I was very upset that she actually followed me to South Africa. But I was determined that my mission was going to be fruitful.

On that faithful Saturday, I was prayed for by Alph Lukau. When I got to the hotel room, I felt a heavy presence of God. I was so happy, and my spirit was so joyous. Before I laid down to sleep, I prayed to God to show me the purpose for my existence. I told God that I wanted to know more about myself, I wanted to know why I was being followed and monitored. I heard the voice of God very loudly, and he said to me, why not pray that you get to know me? I said oh ABBA Father! I thought I knew who God is, but no, I didn't. And ABBA continued to speak to me that night, He told me if I get to know Him, I will discover who I am and the purpose for my existence.

Hearing the voice of God is the most important thing that can ever happen to any child of God, and I know this because, whenever I hear his voice, it changes everything.

The next day was the Sunday service, and Alph Lukau talked about knowing God, he talked about a kind of knowledge of God that comes with an experience of the true God. It was as if God continued the conversation I had with Him in the hotel room through the voice of this great man of God. My life took a new turn, I had encountered God on this visit.

Alph Lukau during prayer time that Sunday, came to where I was knelling, and blew some hot air upon my head. I was dizzy for few seconds, and he turned around the second time and blew more hotness on my head. I lost my ground, but I was kneeling down. I embraced the anointing and that encounter. And it did prepare me for the new level of revelations.

When I got back home, I was like a newborn person. Not because I heard the voice of God, but I also got a confirmation about what God was saying to me.

The very night that I got back, I had another dream. In this dream, I was walking on a street, and that priest who had terrorized me in the dreams saw me coming, he led the people he had with him through another route, and we parted ways, I woke up. I was excited and I laughed so much. Don't you know who God is? And don't mess with my God. The one I just encountered; he is a jealous God! Exactly what I said when I got out of bed.

I continued to follow Alph Lukau on YouTube and listened to all his messages.

More things started happening to me. I was seeing and feeling things. I could feel some hot fire go through my body, though it did happen to me in the past, but not in this dimension. Sometimes this fire will be condensed on my palms, my lower back, my belly. Crazy things started happening to me, I could hear God speak more and more.

God would give me instructions and teachings of the word from the Bible, and it continued until God started visiting me in my room. I just kneel down to pray after midnight and I feel some shadow around where I am praying, some fire burning down my body. I began to have consistent conversations with God.

I needed to know more, so I started seeking for more knowledge. The only prayer I prayed most times was the one God gave me in the hotel room. I started crying onto God to reveal himself to me, and to let me know him. The more I cried unto him the more; strange things happened to me.

Then, I decided to go back for another visit to Alph Lukau. The fire he blew into me was still burning, but I needed a top up.

And I begged Chris, if he could let me go, and he did. He loves Alph Lukau, and he saw Alph Lukau display the power of God in a very raw state.

By now I had become Alph Lukau's daughter and he knew me personally. Not only physically, I knew him spiritually too. In the process of visiting Alleluia Ministries, I started seeing things about the Ministry. And God would wake me up to pray for Alph Lukau. Few times, I argued with God that I needed Alph Lukau to pray for me, I was ignorant.

Encountering witchcraft in South Africa

During my second visit to South Africa, God woke me up around 12 midnight, and he told me to pray for Alph Lukau and the ministry. I had the spirit of prayer fall on me, and I started to pray. While I was praying, God opened my eyes physically to see a tower, and this tower had colorful rainbow lights coming out of it.

And God told me that there was a witchcraft gang up against Alph Lukau, and that they were holding meetings as I prayed. He told me what to say as I continued to pray.

I prayed until past 3AM in the morning, then the hotel phone rang, it was the guy at reception, he told me that some people had called the hotel, that my prayer was disturbing them. He told me to pray gently. I am not a loud person, and I stayed in a hotel apartment just sitting on one corner of the bed praying.

I continued praying because the fire of prayer was still all over me. By 6AM, I heard God tell me to stop. I rounded up my prayers and took a bath. I just wanted to eat breakfast, then go to sleep. My flight was that evening and I needed to rest before heading to the Airport. As I got ready to leave the hotel room, the door was jammed. I tried everything I could to open the hotel door, nothing worked. I called the receptionist, and he sent a maintenance guy to try to unlock the door from outside. This guy tried all the keys, almost 180 keys, and not one worked. He used other mechanism, which didn't work either.

And the guy said to me that he had worked in this hotel for the past 18 years, he had never experienced a thing like this. He said the only option was to use a saw to cut part of the door where the key jammed so I could at least get out of the room. This was already after two hours of trying different methods.

Once he sawed the door to the corner, I was able to get out of the room.

At the breakfast table, God spoke to me, he said I disrupted their activities, so they locked me in. Even though God was telling me so many things about myself, I believed him, but I wasn't convinced.

When I returned from that trip to South Africa, I had a dream that night. In this dream, the lady that I initially lived in her house in USA, the one that I stopped talking to because of the dreams I had about her trying to hurt me, came into my dream and this time around, she had five other women with her. In this dream, I packed my car somewhere and as I was trying to buy some groceries; immediately I came outside to get to my car, I saw her landing from the air. She was levitating, including the women that were with her. And they stopped in front of me, and while she was confronting me about something, the other five women pushed my car into a ditch hitting another car that was packed beside me.

When I turned around to see what had just happened, I was furious, and I went after them; they ran like little chicks. And I woke up. I understood later from God that they were told about what I did in South Africa, so they came to fight, they have a network.

God began to take me deeper into understanding witchcraft and how they operate, that was the beginning of my known encounters with witches trying to kill me. Not only did they intensify their attacks, they would come in groups of six or more sometimes.

God started to equip me more and more. Not only did I know them, and how they operate, he also began to open my eyes to see when they arrange to attack men of God, and he would ask me to pray. Especially for Alph Lukau, he had so much witchcraft attacks. Sometimes God will take me into the Church, and he would show me those who were witches sitting in the Church. How do you start telling a man like Alph Lukau that witches were attending his Church services.

Assigned Death Date

February 2, 2020 was a date that was picked by the witches to kill me, the witches wanted me dead. They no longer want me initiated into their group, I was terrorizing them, and limiting their activities. They wanted me dead. On that date 2/2/2020, I was asleep, but I was uncomfortable, so I woke up to pray. While I was praying, I went into a trance. I found myself in a very big hotel, more like a five-star hotel, and I was given a suite on the third floor. You remember my sister's friend that I said led me to a mortuary when I was heavily pregnant? She was the one who came to the suite. She told me that there was a surprise birthday party going on in ballroom around the lobby for me. She told me they had wanted to surprise me. I walked out of the suite with my daughter and I was holding my daughter, I was leaning down to fix my daughter's pant while arguing with her. I told her I wasn't born in February, and I wanted to know who was throwing a surprise party for me when my birthday is not anyway close to that month? While I was finishing up that statement, the next thing I saw was a headless hand around her. This hand picked her up and threw her across the lobby from the third floor. She laid there motionless. I was so afraid, and I said to myself "what am I going to say, they are going to accuse me of killing her". I hurriedly made an exit using the escalator and immediately I got to the lobby where her body laid flat on the floor, I saw her fellow women. Those who sent her, my sister and their other accomplices who were also top women. They gathered around her, asking her what happened. She looked at me still not moving; but breathing heavily. She told them to ask me what happened?

All of them were staring at me angrily; I told them that I was talking to her and suddenly she was on the floor. She told them that wasn't what happened, she was too tired to speak. I started making my way up to the receptionist to see how they could help her, and I woke up.

Later that day, God told me that the birthday party was a death party. He said to me that whenever witches organize a party for you especially a birthday celebration, it's usually a way of bidding you good-bye.

I am not sure if this woman would ever try to come around me again because the last try, she was lucky to make it out alive. Anyway, there are many other encounters with witches that this book cannot contain.

Encountering Mariners and Occultism

My growth in God was becoming so rapid, and not only do I have dreams in advanced state, but I started to see myself going into prisons where people were locked up, and I would rescue them. I was rescuing people locked up in the witchcraft prisons under the water.

On one of those occasions, the Lord sent me somewhere on a mission. I was with a great speed, running, I didn't know where I was going to, but a voice was leading me. Snakes forcefully flew out of the bushes trying to stop me, and I dodged them while running. The next thing I remember was returning back from this journey. Yes, I went to that place, for some reason God blocked out that information from me. I just remembered my going there with a great speed, and while I was returning, God took me through another route. This route had two major oceans; one on my right, and another on my left with a straight little road in the middle. While I was also running, coming back from that journey, the ocean on my left hand roared at me and rose up forming a shape of a person, and the ocean on my right joined in the roaring. Rising up and forming a shape of a person as well.

Suddenly, a force lifted me above these two human shaped water spirits as they tried to join together to swallow me. Before ever they could meet together, I was up above them, and I watched both of them joining together while I was up in the sky. The one thing that came out of my mouth was "Jesus, please don't drop me, I can't swim deep". Once I said that, I found myself in my room. That was an intense journey, but it wasn't done. I have had many other encounters, swimming down in the deep oceans to rescue people locked up in depth of marine prisons.

Once these encounters began to happen, the occult world came at me.

I was in my room one night, it was about midnight, though I was on my bed, I wasn't sleeping. And suddenly I saw a shadow walk into my room to the side I was on, he started to lift my body physically to take me away. My body was like a hard rock, so he was sweating trying to lift my body. He tried few more times, and I yelled at him to get out of my room, and he flew out speedily.

The Spirit of God told me that these things happen to people, they sleep and die in their sleep because people take them away. It doesn't mean that everyone who died was taken away by these devilish people. Certain people die and people around them just know that it's not a natural death.

On one other occasion, I had a man stand by my window, and before he came, I got a tap on my shoulder and I was told I have a visitor. The person that tapped me on my shoulder (I believe was an angel of God) told me the name of the man, and the purpose which he came for. He wanted to stop my heart or take it away; more like an undertaker. When, he approached I felt his pressure from the window where he stood and reaching towards my heart. I wrestled with him, and cast fire on him, then he disappeared. He tried two more times that very night, and the last time he tried, he got injured. That was the last time, he attempted my house.

One afternoon, I was taking a nap, and someone walked into my room, and kept trying to attack me, but couldn't. He came in with a female body, an old friend of mine, while pretending to be a friend, suddenly I heard what his real name was, and immediately I called him by that name, he turned violent. He jumped on my bed, tried to bite me on my stomach, I knocked him off, and he disappeared.

I began to understand that my life is not solely about me, I was created to help save lives, but the devil wants me, because he wants lives destroyed, and he wants to use the same purpose why I live, against many, but God said no to the devil.

The devil then said if he can't have me, he would kill me, a process he has worked hard at. The only thing he didn't know; he will have to ask permission from God. No one can kill me, not him, not his agents. If he could, he would have killed me by now. Yes, before I wrote this book. That is what they do most of the time. If the Illuminati can't have you, they kill you off. Illuminati and Free masons are pretty much the same, there are the same brotherhood, just different styles of devilish worship.

Encounter with the moon

I was in a dream seeing the catholic church where I grew up. The local catholic church called the Sacred Heart of Jesus Parish, where I saw the face of Jesus as a child? that was where I found myself. They had something going on like a bazaar. People were selling food like a normal bazaar at the Catholic Church. While some were selling food, others were buying food and eating right there.

Suddenly I looked up at the sky, and I saw a full moon. This full moon had a lizard standing close to her. The lizard had wings and could also fly standing.

I saw the lizard talking with the moon; as if it was giving the moon an update. Once the lizard was done talking with the moon, it moved and started flying back into the area where the church bazaar was holding.

There was a woman whose table I was standing by and observing what was happening. I was considering what type of food she sold to people, and why people traded at her table more than the others. There was also a man who was eating at the table. The lizard from the moon flew towards this woman's table and spoke to her. Both of them were communicating and as the lizard was about to move, I told the lizard to get out.

The lizard was mad that I spoke to it and flew across my neck area and I felt it's wing go by as it flew off. My eyes popped open. Oh my, what a dream!

Now, you will recall that woman that I said forced me to drink the dirty water from that kettle, slapping me in the process? She is popularly known as Nwanyi Achara Layout in Enugu. I heard that she moved to the Holy Ghost cathedral in Enugu, where she uses the church hall to pray for people.

The mystery behind this dream is this, that woman is associated with a power from the moon. She has some principalities that she works with which is that flying lizard.

The church is the Catholic Church, and many things go wrong with people's destinies as they eat the food from the table of whoever the agent of the power of darkness is manifesting under. That woman was among those who did the selling, and her witchcraft power is from the moon.

The moon

When God created the two great lights back in Genesis 1:16! The sun is a male, to rule by day, and the moon the female, the lesser light to rule by night. Everything God created, were in form of male and female. there was nothing that He made that was alone. He made them male and female. If you look at psalm 19:5 David described the sun as a bridegroom coming out of his chamber.

Additionally, when God created the two lights, he said let them be for signs, seasons, years, days and months. The moon is female in the spiritual realm; and is responsible for heavy witchcraft attacks that happens on the earth. The moon plays an important role in the manifestation of seasons (psalm 104:19), and anyone who wants to manipulate or control anybody's seasons through witchcraft, uses the moon's power.

Just to clear up your anxiety, the moon is a female spirit, and rules over the night.

The moon also has a strong power and is the origin of every witchcraft power, the moon is where witchcraft derives its power.

You see, in Catholic Church when people count the beads they call rosary, they are contacting the power from the moon, and people often say the rosary has power, of course it does; the question is, where is the power coming from? It's from the moon, and it is a witchcraft power.

This is why you could see a witch carry a long rosary and moving in and out of the Church.

Additionally, the bazaar going on in churches is a means to exchange witchcraft powers. This was exactly what got Jesus very angry, when he entered the temple court and drove out those who were buying and selling sacrificial items and money exchangers saying; "My house shall be called a house of prayer…"(Mathew 21:12-13). He did that because, in the process of people buying and selling, other hidden witchcraft activities were going on.

Islam

Have you noticed the Islamic symbol? What do you see on it? The moon and a star close together, being married to each other? That symbol is simply telling you that someone who was in contact with the moon, gave birth to Islam. Every person born on the earth, has a star that represents them; and whoever gave birth to Islam, was in touch with the moon, or better said, was married to the moon.

When Jesus was born, a star was seen represented in the heavens. Everyone who has breath in them has a star that represents them in the heavenly realm. Don't be deceived, everyone is a star, some just shine brighter than others.

Whenever witches want to mess with you, all they do is locate your star, and seat around the moon to interact with your destiny, that's where they change your seasons. Whenever you continue to go in circles of poverty, or any form of cycle in life, it is because someone is messing with your seasons, and that person is probably a witch.

Have you also seen the Islamic beads? What's the difference between that bead and the rosary? The power is from the same source. The moon's power is like the power of the mind, that's why whenever witchcraft wants to mess with you, it will alter your state of mind, your reasoning and your mental health. That's why when you see people acting crazy, some say they are lunatics, which is of the moon or relating to the moon. Because the moon has strong powers and witchcraft uses this power to mentally oppress their victims.

Halal

the word "Hala" is a female Arabic Name which means " a halo or an aura of light around the moon".

Halal means a worship to a god, a sacrifice or an obeisance to a god. Whenever foods are sacrificed to any god, it is a total worship to that god, and when you eat the food or meat, you are saying to that god that you surrender to its total ownership of your life.

When you take an animal or food, and you make the halal pronouncements which are also incantations, you are saying you sacrificed these foods to the aura around the moon, and you are asking the light around the moon to become your light. This light around the moon therefore becomes your light, to control your seasons, by controlling your own light which is the illumination that occurs in your mind.

Remember I said earlier, that whoever gave birth to Islam was in contact or in marriage with the moon. And you remember also that I said the moon was created to influence and control seasons, and that is the reason why when people act crazy, they say, is it a full moon?

This is also a serious outcome when people eat halal food. The meat is sacrificed to the god of the moon, along with those incantations that they make when they slaughter the animals.

People on the other hand, when they eat these halal meat or food, submit themselves under allegiance to the god which the meat has been sacrificed to. They submit themselves to be controlled by this god, and the way it controls them is by controlling the way they think. It controls their thought process, thereby controlling their seasons. This is why, no matter what you do except by God's divine interventions, these set of people have strong mindsets and believe in what they believe in.

Do you remember the story of Jezebel and the prophets of Baal? Jezebel was the moon goddess, and for her to stay in control, she had hundreds of prophets who ate at her table daily. She literally fed these prophets of Baal everyday (1 Kings 18: 19). Guess what kind of food she fed them? Halal of course. She fed them meals sacrificed to Baal, and in turn had their souls and minds controlled. How do you get a regular person who is not under spell to cut themselves open crying unto Baal to come down and eat a sacrifice they prepared for him?

Do you know what happened to those prophets of Baal? Jezebel was absent, and Baal usually does not respond to regular sacrifices. Baal responds to human sacrifices, and the goddess needs to be around, though they were cutting up themselves, they needed to be lit on fire for Baal to respond. In this case, the goddess, Jezebel herself was absent.

Talk to a Catholics about letting the rosary go, they will face you with a strong fight and argue with their last breath. This is because their minds are controlled through the counting of those beads.

The Catholic Church

If we follow the origin of the Catholic church as argued through history that it was born by the first pope saint Peter, we will also remember that the church was born by the Holy Ghost on the day of Pentecost. You remember in the book of the Acts of the Apostles Chapter 2:1-4, how the Holy Ghost came upon them like a cloven tongue of fire, they all were filled with the Holy Ghost and spoke in new tongues, that was the beginning of the promise of the Church. Then in Acts 2:14-41; after Apostle Peter's sermon, as much as three thousand souls believed in Jesus Christ and were Baptized. This gave birth to the Church of Jesus Christ and after several centuries, would emerge as Roman Catholic Church.

The Catholic church is a universal church. The devil saw the power of the Eucharist in the Catholic church, and how the church was spreading like wildfire, he found a loophole and introduced idolatry and witchcraft into the catholic church. One of the forms of the idolatry and witchcraft in the church is the adherence to the rosary.

If you haven't noticed the devilish trend against the church of our Lord Jesus Christ from the very beginning and you follow your Bible and history well, you will understand what I am trying to say.

What happened to Solomon's temple in Jerusalem and the church of believers in Ephesus that captured Apostle Paul's epistles? The al-Aqsa Mosque sits on the Temple Mount (yes on Solomon's Temple) and Ephesus is in present day Turkey which had become Islamized. Anywhere you see the church of Christ making any form of progress, watch out for those who stand to eliminate Christianity. Why do you think that so many Christians lose their lives in the hands of extreme Islamist groups? Just ponder.

The reason is because there are certain groups that the lady of the kingdom and satanic forces have raised to eliminate Christianity.

In November of 2015, Pope Francis visited a mosque at Bangui, in the Central African Republic and told them that Christians and Muslims are brothers and should act as such! Really, act as such. Islam categorizes Christians as infidels and equates them to unbelievers who are to be beheaded. Additionally, the spread of Islam by Jihad speaks of a different testimony.

Furthermore, the apostle Paul in 2 Thessalonians 3: 2 implored Christians to pray for them to be delivered from evil and wicked men; for all have not faith. Adding to that, Hebrews 11:6 says that without faith, it is impossible to please God and as Christians, our faith and salvation rests on the finished works of Jesus Christ, which Islam does not accept. Something does not sound right with the pronouncement of the Pope. He must be deriving his authority from elsewhere but the Christian Bible. In addition, Romans 8:14 says that as many as are led by the spirit of God, they are the sons of God. Something must have led the Pope to say what he said and still says. For sure, it is not the Holy Spirit. Lest I forget, the Pope is the head of the Catholic Church. I would rather leave the Pope to his pronouncements. The truth remains that Satan has always used Islam against Christianity, and that is where the antichrist will rise from.

Nonetheless, if anyone can take hold of your mind and your thought process, then he/she can control your entire life and your seasons.

The Queen of Heaven

The Queen of heaven is also known as the lady of the kingdom who was addressed in the book of Isaiah 47. If you look at the book of Isaiah

47:1, Isaiah called out the Queen of heaven, who is also known as the virgin daughter of Babylon and the daughter of the Chaldeans. She is portrayed as tender and delicate, but obviously, you could see how the Bible addressed her. She occupies a throne, which is located on the moon, and she rules many from there.

Examining her a bit further; why was she referred to as the daughter of the Chaldeans?

The Chaldeans are the present-day Iraq which is a strong Muslim country. To further deepen your knowledge of the relationship between the rosary and the Islamic beads, I would like you to know that the origin of the rosary could be traced back to the Islamic beads and to Fatima. Additionally, it would interest you to know that Fatima was the daughter of prophet Muhammed.

The rosary prayed in the catholic church and the Islamic beads, both come from the same source of power, and there is no difference at all.

Let me help you a little further, when you study the man Abraham in the book of Genesis, you will understand that he and his father were moon worshippers. It was in the process of Abraham's deep moon worship that God called him, and told him to leave his father's house and the idolatry to the Land He would show him. (Genesis 12:1)

Previously in Genesis 11:31, Terah Abram's father took him, his wife Sarai, and Lot his grandson who was Abram's brother, and they were going to sojourn into Canaan. But I want you to pay a special attention to where they were sojourning from; the Ur of the Chaldees. Does that ring a bell? The Chaldeans which is the present day Iraq originated from the Abram's father Ur of the Chaldees. And they were known for gross idolatry, worship of the Moon.

This virgin daughter of Babylon and daughter of the Chaldeans is a moon goddess, even though most of the time she appears to be tender and delicate as the book of Isaiah describes, but her tenderness could be associated to the depth of her deceitful characteristics. Her level of deceit can be seen in her delicate and tender appearance.

Check your bible very well, the word "Hail Mary" is not anywhere in it. What the Angel (Gabriel) who was a messenger of God said to her was "Hail" which is a Greek word for "Chairo" same word as "Greetings "or better "Hello" it's also the word for "Rejoice or Be Glad" The Angel said "Greetings" to Mary, but he didn't use it in the same context that the Catholic uses it when they count the beads.

God would never intend for man to go through anyone to reach Him the Father, except through his Son Jesus Christ, and this is why Jesus warned us multiple times that He is the way, the truth and life, and no one can get to the Father except through him (John 14:6). Anyone who tries to enter in through any other means or door is a thief, according to Jesus. And he went further to characterize the devil as the thief who only comes to steal, kill and destroy.

Anyone who is trying to convince you that you need to beg Mary, who on other hand begs Jesus to have mercy on you is deceiving you, and is also deceived.

Can I tell you the truth? Jesus for this whole purpose of preventing idolatry broke this tie with Mary before his death on the cross. Do you remember when Jesus turned to his mother Mary and said "Woman behold thy son", and to John the beloved "Behold thy mother" (John 19:26-27)? What he did there was to break this tie, because he knew that people would automatically idolize his mother if he didn't set the record right. Jesus knew that in heaven, there is only one throne, and only one king; The Father. There are only Twenty four elders surrounding the throne of God according to Revelation 4. There is no other position for a woman called the mother of God in heaven, because there is nothing like the mother of God in heaven; God has no beginning and will have no end, without father and without mother...(Hebrew 7:3).

Jesus was 100% man (Hebrew 2:16-17) and also 100% God (John 1:1-2, 14).

Mary was 100% man, and 0% God, she was just a channel and a vehicle through which God came into the earth as a man, just for the total purpose of redeeming the man that he created in his image.

Check the scripture very well, after Jesus resurrected from the dead, you never heard about Mary his mother again. It's not because she wasn't important any more, but because, God tried to prevent the idolizing of Mary the mother of Jesus.

Yes! Mary had her purpose in the kingdom, but that purpose was to carry the child of the Holy Ghost, a seed of a woman into the world; that she completed very well. But Satan knows that man is always prone to idolatry, and when he found that loop hole in Fatima, he introduced it to that vulnerable population.

Have you ever asked yourself this question, or perhaps out of your own ignorance skipped to ask yourself this question? The image that you see circulating as the mother of Jesus and carrying the infant Jesus, who created that image, and how do you validate that it was indeed the image of the mother of Jesus holding him at birth. And you would also read some stories in Catholic church such as the coronation of the blessed virgin Mary; a feast that is celebrated by the Catholic church, would you for once question where her throne is? And who crowned her? If you look at the Bible very well, the book of Revelation 4 & 5 discussed in detail the Coronation of Jesus Christ, and Jesus actually addresses Himself as the One who sits upon the Throne in Revelation 3:21.

For this purpose, to avoid idolatry did God forewarned his people in Exodus 20:4 "You shall not make for yourself an image in the form of anything in heaven above or on the earth beneath or in the waters below"

Literally, the scripture said "An Image" weather an image that looks like Jesus or like his mother, it doesn't matter. The next verse Exodus 20:5 tells you that this action of creating an image either ignorantly or knowingly of such image and bowing before it, is a highly punishable sin for up to third and fourth generation. "You shall not bow down to them or worship them; for I, the LORD your God, am a jealous God, punishing the children for the sin of the parents to the third and fourth generation of those who hate me"

Could this be the reason Satan is so strong in leading people through idol worship, to draw God to Jealous, and to tie generations down?

The Illuminati

The Illuminati is a clandestine group, who pay obeisance to Satan. They believe they have the power to do anything. They have been given this false sense of entitlement from Satan to do anything they want and to go into anywhere they want.

This group have the elites, they have access to billionaires who sponsor their wickedness.

They believe they own America and they also have groups all over the world.

The Illuminati is a group that believe they need to have the highest quality of individuals in their group. They want to control power and it's access; this is why when they pick any interest in you, they will monitor you, track your moves to the latest update. If they see any form of light in you, they hack you down to their group. Satan has been able to convince them and has stolen their souls. Their footprints are known everywhere they enter, because they operate in a certain way.

The Illuminati will negotiate with you if you are gifted and exceptional in your talents. They will offer you everything except peace. They will give you money, power and fame; but you will still suffer that incompleteness that every one of them feel. The access to the illuminati is very limited. They only go for the exceptionally talented and gifted individuals.

You would recall that, Satan told Jesus to bow down and worship him and he will give him the keys to the kingdom of this world. That's what the Illuminati does to their members. It is the same thing that Satan spoke to the woman at Eden. Satan spoke to Jesus and tried to negotiate with him in the wilderness. This same Satan is the one negotiating with many around the world for a worship. The only thing is that he is not telling them that in the process of you bowing to worship him, he steals from you. Yes, he is not a fool, the man that God created and gave power over Satan is the one who has been foolish enough to switch his place with Satan. Man is above Satan and not the reverse.

Satan plays on people's ignorance. He knows predominantly people lack knowledge. That is why the Bible says in Hosea 4: 6, my people are destroyed for the lack of knowledge. Satan knows that many don't know that they have superiority over him. He is a fallen angel, though anointed, but in no way above man. The problem he encountered in heaven with God was because he wanted to be positioned above man, to be a god to man. He wanted to be like the most-High (God). He is still the same old guy, even though he manifests in different ways.

Anyway, Illuminati means the control over one's mind and light. Illuminati takes over your natural light (your mind), and gives you a different kind of light, so you can reason like the devil, a perverted light.

You remember that Lucifer means the light bearer? he was created with so much illumination, but he perverted his light through sin, his light became darkness. Darkness is not really an absence of light. It just means a lesser light.

When you get to the book of Genesis 1:5, God during the time of creation, called the day light, and the night He called darkness. It then means that darkness means a lesser light. You can also verify this statement by reading down to Genesis 1:16. God created two lights, the greater light to control the day, and the lesser to rule the night. This lesser light means you are not able to see clearly.

When you look at the book of John 1:4, it says that "In him (Jesus) was life, which was the light of men" This then tells you that man has a different kind of light that he bears. Lucifer, the bearer of lesser light. He knows his light is lesser than that of man, he knows this very truth, the light in man when he was created, was the same light of God. This light was what Jesus was referring to when he said that " I am the light of the world: whoever follows me will never walk in darkness..." (John 8:12).

Permit me to say that the life of Jesus (light) is in everyone who enters the world (John 1:9), but how you respond to it and activate it is totally dependent on your choice.

Unfortunately, many have chosen to follow the lesser light which is what Lucifer bears. It's a form of darkness. He; the devil knows that if you ever get to discover your kind of light, the light of God which he gave to everyone (whoever gets born into the world), you will defeat him by discovering his perversions.

I said everyone who enters the world by birth has this great light in them. The problem is, you will need to choose who to connect to; this turns on your light. This is why the serpent went to the woman at the garden and corrupted her light. The Bible said she was deceived (1 Timothy 2:14). Have you asked yourself why the serpent went to the woman and not the man? It was because the man had more-light than the woman, he was the one God gave the information regarding the tree of the knowledge of good and evil. But the man did a poor job, he didn't enlighten his wife, he gave her insufficient information about the tree of knowledge of good and evil. How did I know this? Because the woman said to the serpent, they were not to touch the tree, and that wasn't what God said to Adam. (Genesis 3:3).

If you follow God to the book of Genesis 2:17, He told Adam not to eat the fruit of that tree, and He also told him the consequences of not obeying Him. Let's get back to the topic of discussion.

In the book of John 1:9, the true light lights every man coming into the world. It means regardless of what kind of family you were born into, there is that true light that you were created with. You will need to discover it for yourself. It's just too bad that Satan doesn't give people a chance to discover the true light, he bombards them with deception, and they are not able to discover the light they were born with.

You may then ask, what does eating-something got to do with your mind? And I will like to ask you why did God put what you should not eat in the midst of the garden? And why did Adam eyes open to notice that they were naked?

Because, the switch to controlling what you eat is in your mind; if you can control what you eat, you can control your mind and what you do. Why did Satan say to Jesus first " turn the stone into bread" to prove that he is the son of God? What does being the Son of God got to do with bread and stone? Who are you listening to? Anyone who is able to control your mind, can control what you eat. So, the devil chooses this-tactics just to get hold or gain control over one's mind.

Have you noticed that people who have no control over the body, and what they can eat also have other psychological problems?

No covenant is established without a meal. Whenever you agree with someone, you eat to seal the agreement. This is what the devil does, offer you a meal, it's a form of idolatry.

When Jesus was about to enter a new covenant, he broke bread and wine with his disciples.

No form of witchcraft or occultic initiation is established without a meal. If the devil wants to initiate you into his kingdom, it doesn't happen without you eating or drinking something. Ask anyone who has ever been initiated into the occultism or the witchcraft world, you get to eat or drink something.

The eating or the drinking of whatever it is that you are given, is a way of you submitting your mind to total control. Your mind is where the light bulb is, and for the devil to control your reasoning, your thoughts which in turns controls your life, he needs you to hand over the light switch to him. You do this by submitting to whatever he asked you to do.

The Bible said that angels are ministering spirits and are sent forth to minister to those who will inherit salvation. (Hebrew 1:14). If you understand this, you wouldn't trade your position of power with Satan. The devil is superior in knowledge than the people he has stolen from. (Jesus told his disciples to be wise as the serpent) Mathew 10:16. That should educate you more that the devil, the serpent or Satan is not a fool. He is very calculative, and a very successful merchant from the beginning. People are selling their souls to him because they are ignorant.

Ignorance is the worst enemy of man, what you don't know fights you and can kill you.

In other words, Satan the god of the Illuminati, is manifesting and he is forceful at it. He has agents all over the world, and they are able to track anyone down.

You see, the Illuminati is the same Jezebel spirit that reigned in the times of the Bible. It's very dangerous at locating prophetic ministries and has been successful at bringing many of them down. The Illuminati hates prophets because of one thing; the power to reveal things. An accurate prophet of God knows the footsteps and prints of the Illuminati. This is why the Illuminati love to stay around prophets, to negotiate with them.

Now, let's look at the word "Illuminate". The Oxford dictionary says it means to make something visible or bright by shining light on it.

Now, that's what prophets do. They reveal the minds of God to the people. Satan also has chosen his own group of prophets to illuminate his own plans and help propel them to the world. That's just what the Illuminati does; to show off Satan and his plans.

You can't fight Illuminati if God has not equipped you to, but you can resist them as a child of God, if you understand your place and they would flee from you.

Unfortunately, many of the subsidiaries of Illuminati have been implanted into churches to ruin the things of God. If you are a prophetic ministry, they send people after you to negotiate with you. This is why many who started as true prophets of God have somewhere along their journey fallen into the trap and become one of them. This is why you have many occultists imposing as pastors and prophets; they started very well and on a good note, but because of their lusts, got entangled with Illuminati.

Balaam, the prophet who was hired by Balak to curse the people of God, was a true prophet who heard from God. He was made an offer very lustfully enticing, he became a false prophet; so is everyone who has been enticed by the devil. He gives you what you cannot say no to, if you are controlled by your lusts.

When you look properly through the Bible, you will see from Adam in Genesis, to Jesus; how Satan negotiated with many of the prophets. You

The Devil of America Wants Me!

know, Satan will not make you an offer if you have nothing. He was a trafficker from the beginning; the offer he is making to you is connected to taking away what you already have and using it for himself. Everything and everyone he is trading with today all have those God given potentials in them, they just didn't know they did.

A false prophet like I said, was once a true prophet who Satan offered money and fame in exchange for his gifts.

Talk about the Illuminati sending women over to churches, the daughters of Jezebel, are in churches to seduce the prophets and bring them to their knees. This is why some prophets are not able to see anymore. God does not take any gift he has given to anyone (the free gifts of God are without repentance; Romans 11:29), but the devil can steal your gifts. He sends women into churches, what they do is seduce the man of God and take his gifts away from him. He wakes up and unable to prophesy anymore because he cannot see anything. This is how many of them got entangled with Satan. Then he makes them an offer they won't resist, because they need to keep up the game.

Encountering Chadwick Bozeman 10/2/2020

What happened to Chadwick Bozeman?

The death of Chadwick was disturbing, it lingered in my heart for some time, I was not happy. When I get troubled this way, sometimes even without asking God what happened, he can show me what actually happened. I wasn't asking for what happened to him, I knew it wasn't ordinary, but I wasn't happy that it happened.

On this date, I was in a dream; I was taken into a location where people were partying so hard. I looked past the party hall, and there was an open space inside the house, and I saw the Wakanda's guy that died, Chadwick Bozeman. He was wrestling with another man, a white guy average in height, just about his height. This white guy looked young too. He suddenly kicked this white guy who tried to kick him back; but didn't kick him hard enough. It was as if he was teaching this white guy how to fight! He said to this guy who was wrestling with him, "feel free to kick hard" Immediately, this guy kicked him really hard on his stomach area, Puss and Margot leaked out of his stomach. I was staring at him as well as others around, who were also watching what was happening to him. He immediately said, "its ok, its ok" because this white guy became worried from the look on his face, and he tried to help Chadwick clean the puss and the maggot off his skin. But the more he cleaned it, the more it leaked out. As I walked away from that scene, I met the people partying inside, I remember the song they were dancing to as I walked pass the hall towards the outside, I woke up.

Interpretation:

Chadwick wrestled with a certain group in Hollywood. He was given an option to surrender his soul if he wanted to be a hero in Hollywood. He interacted with them, some of them were his friends, but he wanted to be his own person.

Chadwick's death wasn't ordinary, the puss coming out of his stomach is a sign that it was not a natural thing. Puss and Maggot don't belong on the stomach area. It is usually a wicked attack from the witchcraft world. Whatever Chadwick suffered was not natural, there was more to it. What I am not sure of was the kick on the belly. Whoever it was that kicked him on the belly was responsible for making the puss and Margot come out. This guy who was wrestling with him was not known to me and another thing that shocked me was that he didn't fight this guy. He just said it was ok, and he tried to clean the puss off.

In America, you have to belong somewhere to get to the top. In Hollywood especially you cannot be a hero and enjoy heroism if you haven't either paid obeisance to God above or mostly to the devil. The devil of Hollywood wouldn't want you to get there, and if you decide to get yourself there, you must continue whatever you did to get there to stay there. To some, it warrants handing over their souls to the devil, to others you will have to work out your salvation.

Whichever you choose will determine your outcome. If the devil has an interest in you because of your God given talents, if there is something you carry that he sees, a light that is brighter than others, he comes after you. He tries to negotiate with you, to buy you over, meaning to offer you something you don't know you have, in exchange for your soul.

If you fall to his traps, he takes what's in you, perverts it and uses it to destroy you and the world around you.

Looking at the Bible from the beginning, he did that to the woman at the garden of Eden, and her husband fell for it. He tried it with Jesus, but he failed. He has the same tactics and tricks. He is a trafficker, that's what he did from the beginning.

CHAPTER TWELVE

More Encounters

M Y ENCOUNTERS WITH GOD GREW stronger and stronger. Sometimes I would have an encounter where God would use Alph Lukau to lay hands on me to strengthen me.

But I needed answers and I needed someone who would be able to at least explain or give me an information regarding the things I was physically encountering. Certain times my eyes would open to see things written in coded forms. I would see these things dropping from the sky to the earth, but yet no explanations.

Although the Spirit of God was doing a lot of teachings most times, I desired to learn more. I asked God about going to a theology school and God asked me some deep questions.

God asked me who taught Jesus? Or to bring it closer to my understanding, who taught Moses the things he wrote about creations? And I understood what God meant. He didn't condemn the school of theology or learning, but he didn't want me going through that route.

You have to remember that I had already gone through the school of ministry and I had studied all those kinds of stuff. Meanwhile, when I was serving at the Nigerian church, my pastor had also sent a few of us to some kind of school of ministry. We graduated and got certificates, but I really didn't understand Christianity until God spoke to me about getting to know him.

I realized that many who walk around professing church and doing

Church really have not known God. Anyone who ever encounters God cannot live a normal life.

Encountering God in the place of Prayer

In the process of praying for a mentor, someone I could relate to, I had an encounter.

In this dream, I was on my knees praying and my son was also praying with me. I was on my knees just asking God for a mentor. While I was there, someone walked into the room. I couldn't see this person; but I could see a shadow like that of water. He was in form of a substance that was colorless. He said to me, "Get up and hold my hands" and I said to him, but I can't see your hands. He said to me "reach for my hands and I will hold you"

While kneeling down I reached for his hands and immediately my hand bumped into his hands; these hands were huge and soft at the same time. He grabbed my two hands and pulled me up and then threw me up to the sky while holding me. And he gently dropped me back on the floor standing. I was overwhelmed, but I was more conscious of who saw what had just happened to me.

I didn't pay attention to who it was that lifted me off my feet and I didn't bother to ask him who he was, I was just looking around to see if anyone noticed how I was up in the sky and back again.

My eyes caught that of my son, and he said to me, mommy how did you just do that? then I woke up. Now I understood what God was saying. He wants to lead me by Himself, but I was doubtful at times, I would retract from perceiving what God was teaching because they were deep things, and sounded crazy to the human mind, but I still desired to know more.

God began to show me the true spiritual men as I approach them.

After one week of my encounter in the place of prayer, I bumped into a man of God on the internet, when I considered his display of the power of God, I wasn't so attentive to the things he was saying.

Then I was in a dream that night, and this man of God a prophet, came into the place where I was, and he asked me to iron his shirts and went away. And while I stood looking at his shirt I woke up. I knew it was a bad idea to even go close to a person like him. He is probably looking for a servant or he may turn me into one.

God has a way of responding to me, even to my thoughts and imaginations; and I am very appreciative of this, because this to me is a display of how much God loves me, and to the extent he is willing to protect me.

Encounter with My Ancestors

In the process of writing this book, I had an encounter with my ancestors. In this dream, I had finished working and returned home to a house full of ancestors. They were all sitting in my living room and waiting patiently for me to get home. When I entered through the door, I was told by my husband's cousin that people were waiting to talk to me. I went straight to the room where they were, and I couldn't recognize any one of them. They were group of old men, so old and stricken with age. I greeted them and sat down to hear what they had to say.

One of them turned around to me, with something he had in his hands, it looked like what the Jews would call an ephod. He also had two other wooden crafted staff with him, which he demonstrated with when he was talking to me. What did he say to me?

He said that the ancestors after their meetings and consultations, have decided that I am the right person to be given the office of the chief priest of the gods. Immediately I heard that, I rose up from where I was sitting, and I said; " I am a believer of Jesus Christ and cannot worship any other god". One of them that was seated on the floor rose up, came closer to me, and persuaded me saying " we are not telling you to worship another god, all you will need to do is to communicate with the ancestors and then tell the people what they have said" in other words, be a mediator between the ancestors and the people. He continued to say that it was a general consensus after the consultations that I am the one fit for the office. I insisted that I couldn't be interacting with my ancestors, I told them it is called ancestral worship. They got up and left, and I woke up.

Woah! I said, and I started to pray and cancel every covenant made on my behalf by my ancestors.

While I was praying, I slept off and I was in another dream. In this dream, I had also just returned from work and when I opened the front door, I walked into some ancestral artifacts. Some of them were like masquerade heads and including many other items. And I asked the person I met at the front door, who was also trying to leave my house, what the objects were for? He told me that the ancestors have looked around and they couldn't find anyone who would hold the office of the chief priest in my community, no one was fit for that office. He continued to say that the ancestors decided to leave these items with me, and I could just do whatever I want with them. I got furious and angry and I started to kick them out of my house with my foot. I told him, to come back and take the items back to them, because I am not interested, while kicking the items out of my house, I woke up.

Now, I am thinking, this is serious, but I am happy I told my ancestors I couldn't worship them. I am in love with Jesus Christ. As for me and my household, we will serve the Lord. (Joshua 24:15).

Alph Lukau

Everyone I met or watched on the internet I compared them with Alph Lukau.

You have to understand that's where I had a true encounter and an experience with the voice of God. Not that I didn't hear God before, but my hearing God wasn't as loud as it has become.

Alph Lukau is a man of power, a man endowed with so much grace. Alph is an avenger, he was sent to God's people to do justice in the Kingdom.

You see, Jesus said in the book of Luke 4:18, how the Spirit of the Lord was upon him...and in verse 19 of the same chapter, he concluded with a statement; "To preach the acceptable year of the Lord" (Luke 4:19)That was Jesus ministry on the earth.

Every man endorsed by God is given power to do as it is written of them, in the volume of the book of their lives. This means that there is something you are assigned to do on the earth as a child of God.

Where am I going with this? get to the book of Isaiah 61:2, it is the continuation of what Jesus came to do on earth. He finished his portion and he handed over the baton to his body, the church, to continue from where he stopped. This is why Jesus said greater work shall you do because I go to my father (John 14:12). He wasn't playing with words when he said that, he has greater works here on earth for the church to do.

Part of that greater work is in Isaiah 61:2. "It is an acceptable year of the LORD, and it is also the day of the vengeance of our God; to comfort all that mourn..."

Whenever God wants to avenge Himself, he sends a man that would go for him. Read through the scriptures, God said "vengeance is mine..." (Deuteronomy 35:35) and truly it is. But God cannot avenge Himself on the earth without the use of a man.

There are a set of people who have been called to avenge for God's people, the man Alph Lukau is one of them. This is why the devil hates him so much. He has been given raw power to deal with the devil.

The Hebrew word Yown (The day of) his vengeance as used in Isaiah 61:2 has the same literal meaning as the word for season and times. If God is saying there is an acceptable day, season and time for His vengeance, I think we are in that season.

Alph Lukau, judges the satanic world, and he was empowered to do so. He sends an arrow that does not bend on its way until it hits its targets.

Nonetheless, there is a famous precedence in the court of law, "he who must judge, must also be just" (R v Sussex Justices, ex parte McCathy) 1924. Having said that, if God appoints you an avenger, to bring justice to the church, you must be diligent in doing that, knowing that the devil whom you judge his kingdom is also an accuser, and was also an anointed Cherub.

When you look at the book of Revelation 12:10, it talks about the accuser of the brethren who accused them before God day and night, and how he has been chased down to the earth. And he talked about the woes that the inhabitants of the earth would face, because this accuser knows that he has a short time.

Now, the accuser who was chased down to the earth hasn't ceased to be an accuser, rather he has increased his accusation skills. He accuses God before his people (this is what the Bible calls blasphemy). He mocks God before His people, he tries to make God's people doubt his ability to save, to provide and to protect.

Have you heard the devil speak to you about God? He is very idiotic at it, and he speaks blasphemy. This is why people can open their wide mouths and say if God is real, why the wars, the hurricanes, the hunger, the virus? It's Satan who inspires them to speak these words.

Apart from accusing God before His people, Satan accuses the brethren directly, before their faces.

As a man of power, you never give the devil a chance to taunt you. He throws a bait at you, and you fall for it, and then, he turns around to challenge you about God's given authority and power over him.

How do you have someone cast out the devils that he has been mingling with?

As an avenger, you are equipped with every gadget that you need spiritually. But you must also equip yourself with men who are capable of doing what you do, men who are people of Character.

Looking at David who equipped himself with mighty men of war. One of his men Adino the Eznite slew 800 men in one day. Talk about Eleazar the son of Dodo, just as his last name sounds, he did mighty things in the battlefield; 2 Samuel 23:8-13.

Paul said in 1 Corinthians 6:2, " Do you know that the saints shall judge the world? Are you unworthy to judge the smallest matters?

Meeting Emmanuel Makandiwa

During the early period of the COVID 19 pandemic, I came across this prophet of God Emmanuel Makandiwa on YouTube. There was a short clip where he had prophesied about the pandemic back in 2015. As I watched it, I was amazed at his accuracy. I didn't watch anymore videos about him. I am very careful of what I watch, who I pay attention to; there are many sad things happening in the church of Jesus Christ today.

After one week of watching Makandiwa on YouTube, I had an encounter about him.

In this dream, I was at a penthouse in an open room waiting to see Alph Lukau, this was the third time that I was waiting to see Alph Lukau in my dreams. On two occasions I waited for him to sign my certificate after going through school, but he didn't because he was very busy. I woke up frustrated.

Nonetheless, while I was in this open space in that penthouse waiting to see Alph Lukau, I was also praying on my knees while Alph Lukau was busy with some people.

Suddenly, Emmanuel Makandiwa walked into that room, walked pass Alph Lukau to where I was kneeling, and he told me to follow him. I got up and walked behind him. Immediately we went pass Alph Lukau, I awoke out of this dream.

I didn't need further explanation to know what God was saying, I understood it very clearly.

My supernatural encounter with Emmanuel Makandiwa

On the 7/7/2020, I was in a dream where I was attending a church service, but before the church service, I had seen my uncle who died many years ago. He was like a security guard at the gate of this school where the fellowship was being held. He handed me 9 of $50 notes, I counted the money and it was totaled $450.

Suddenly, I was at the school fellowship hall, and Emmanuel Makandiwa was the guest minister for that day. I took all the money that my uncle gave to me and handed it over to Emmanuel Makandiwa after his ministrations, and as if I was one of the ushers, I had to walk him to his car because I was also carrying some of the gifts that were given to him. The idea was to walk him to the car park, and we were talking while we walked together, I don't remember what the discussions was about. All I remember was asking where he parked his car, which he told me he didn't come with a car.

I had an old Mercedes sedan in this dream, which was parked at the same car park, and I offered to drop him off at the junction where the buses picked up people.

He didn't want me dropping him off, he only asked for the directions to the bus stop. I told him the directions, handed him his gifts that I was carrying, and also a pack of meal prepared for the ministers.

He took those things from me, and handed me his complimentary card, and told me to get his direct number from one of the ministers at the school.

Immediately I turned around again to wave him goodbye, a brand-new Mercedes sedan was parked in front of him, no one was driving it. He entered the Mercedes and started to eat the piece of chicken from the meal plate, and he smiled at me. I was confused, I pondered on who this man was? He just told me he didn't have a car, yet a car which had no driver appeared before him.

Nonetheless, I continued to walk back to the hall where the church service was held. Then I heard some group of students talking about him. One of them that I knew personally said something intriguing, she said it was illegal for him to do what he just did. She said that Makandiwa had just committed an offense called theophany, and she continued to argue with two other students standing with her. They also said that the court will also declare his action illegal. When I walked past where they were standing, I pondered on the word theophany and what they were saying; I have heard it somewhere, that was my thought in this dream. While I pondered on this word, I woke up from this dream. Up until now, I am still seeking for proper interpretation of this dream.

Emmanuel Makandiwa is a man that has brought enlightenment to my many dreams, because he has taught me things that I have searched for. The questions that were unanswered for many years, Makandiwa brought answers. A man that spoke words that lighted up the raw materials God gave to me. He gave me explanations to some of my unsolved mysteries. I thought something had gone wrong with me until I met Emmanuel Makandiwa. Though I haven't met him physically, but I have met him few times in the spiritual realm.

When he talks, you have to know the things he knows to understand him. If not, you would call him illegal like my friends.

The things he speaks, some cannot be found anywhere in the Bible. But you also have to understand that before the Bible, there was no Bible. The things Paul spoke about, where did he get them from?

Yes, we want to be scripturally correct when we share the word of God, but our God is a moving and a quickening Spirit, and if you want everything he tells you to be based on what Paul and other apostles wrote, you will be stuck.

How do you explain to people that when John was told by one of the Elders "Weep not: Behold the lion of the tribe of Judah, the Root of David hath prevailed…" (Revelation 5:5) KJV! In this instance, that one elder that spoke to John was actually King David! What would be your scriptural backing to say this kind of thing except that the Lord revealed it to you.

If you are still confused, how did Jude know that the archangel Michael contended with Satan over the body of Moses in Jude 1: 9; except that it was revealed to him. If you would recall, the Bible expressly said that Moses went up the Mountain, died and was buried there by the lord in the land of Moab (Deuteronomy 32: 50; 34: 6).

Getting back to the issue of the elder who spoke to John; God asked me on one of the days I was having a conversation with Him, regarding the book of Revelation 5:5. He said to me "who was the elder who spoke to John to weep no more?" first I didn't say anything because, I didn't know what the answer was until He told me it was King David.

In my usual self, I pondered on that for a while and although I didn't say anything to God, from my thoughts, He understood I had questions about what He just told me, how can you prove that?

He referred me to the book of Mathew 22:44, when Jesus asked the Pharisees "How then does David in the Spirit call him Lord? Saying: the LORD said to my Lord sit at my right hand…"

God continued to explain to me that when John had his revelation, King David was actually sitting where he was seated when he saw that revelation of God the Father and Jesus.

Who else would have introduced the Lion of the Tribe of Juda and the Root of David better than David himself? Think about that.

In a related dimension, how do you explain to people that the poor girl whose father (Jephthah) sacrificed unto the LORD because he had vowed a vow that whatever comes out first from his door would become a sacrifice unto God, if God gave him victory over the Ammonites. (Judges 11:30-38). In addition, how do you explain that the same girl became Mary the mother of Jesus? How do say that because it wasn't written anywhere in the scriptures. I would like to state that in the book of Malachi 4:5, the Bible said I will send Elijah the prophet before the coming of the great and dreadful day of the lord. Furthermore, Jesus said that Elijah the prophet had come but the Jews did not know it was him (referring to John the Baptist in Matthew 11: 13-14).

Nonetheless, when the Lord was trying to remind me of his faithfulness, He choose to give me the information about Jephthah's daughter and the virgin Mary, the mother of Jesus. The information was just to reinforce that he never forgets a labor of love, and services done in his Kingdom.

God told me that Jephthah's daughter, whom he handed over to the service of God because he had made a vow unto God, died as a virgin in the service of God. He had to return that favor to her by allowing her to become the mother of Jesus.

You remember when she told her father Jephthah to give her two months to bewail her virginity in Judges 12:37? She actually went up and down the mountain as the custom denotes to wail (deep sorrow) that she was going to be a perpetual virgin. God before hand prepared the mother of Jesus in the person of that virgin daughter of Jephthah, a woman who had no sexual contact with any man. A woman who was offered as a sacrifice unto the Lord, but returned to actually carry the son of God. That, which her father did, prepared her to be a woman whose seed would bruise the serpent's head. I would like you to consider her answers to her father in Judges 12:35-37, and compare them to her response when the angel visited her in Luke 1:34 &38, to see the similarity in the way she responded to the things of God.

Now, how would I explain such a thing to someone? They will say you speak illegal things.

Only a certain group of people would understand the things Emmanuel Makandiwa speaks. To others, he is illegal in the things he utters out of his mouth as the voice of God.

How do you explain the things United Kingdom based Prophet Uebert Angel says? How do you explain some of his deep revelations? How he takes the scriptures and brings it to the happenings of today!

There are people who are called to inherit the kingdom of God and they have actually inherited it, along with working for its expansion. These are the set of people, or men and women of God called reapers as Jesus mentioned in Mathew 13:30, where Jesus made an example of kingdom of God and highlighted the role of reapers.

I would like to state that many have been called and out of those who are called, those who take their calling seriously are the few who have been chosen. The chosen are the actual reapers. They are hand-picked and trained differently to be able to separate the tares from the wheat.

You know Jesus said to the servants who asked for permission to root out the tares from the field; "Nay; lest while ye gather up the tares, ye root up also the wheat with them" (Mathew 12:29)KJV.

What Jesus was literally saying here is that there are people who have been trained with special anointing to do this kind of Job, they are called the reapers.

These group are different from the servants who are unskilled. They are unskilled in the sense that they can cause more harm in the field than good.

Servants are not able to do this kind of Job, it's reserved for those who are Sons, the disciples of Jesus Christ, they are called the reapers. They are the true sons of God. Many of those who call themselves men of God do more damage in the kingdom of God than good.

If you look also at the book of John 8:35, Jesus said that servants have no long standing in the house, but sons have. And he took it further to say that only the son can make one free indeed.

It means that there are people who can set you free, and the freedom will be temporarily, short-lived. Only sons have the authority and have inherited the power to make one free indeed. They have the abilities to gather the wheat into the barn of the father without rooting out souls from the kingdom of God. They seek not their own, they seek to manage the father's house properly.

Servants on the other hand render services because they are going to get paid (benefit) for it and are strictly about rendering services for payments which is their rewards.

Unfortunately, in the kingdom of God today, there are more servants than reapers. They are very loud and display what people think are miracles, but at the end the people are still bound and are not free.

Jesus healed people and the Bible actually recorded that they that came were healed. All of them and they that had devils in them had the devils kicked out of their lives in speed. (Luke 4:45). The Bible has no record of where anyone who was healed, lost their healings after Jesus healed them.

I am not sure why many people today are said to lose their healings after a while. It means they received a temporary healing or deliverance.

That is what Jesus was saying when he said that if the son shall set you free, you shall be free indeed. (John 8:32)

If you are a man of God who has inherited the kingdom of God, you will see the devils flee from you, crying out like they did to Jesus.

Now, there are many who are in the kingdom, who have their authority set. Nonetheless, due to sin, they cannot inherit the kingdom of God. Certain level of exercises of power and authority are for the sons of God, the true disciples of our Lord Jesus Christ.

Who is your teacher?

Jesus said in the book of John 8:28b "but my Father hath taught me, I speak these things…". Who is then your teacher? Because the success you will experience in life is dependent on what you have learned from your teacher. Could it be why Jesus was so successful in Ministry that within three years, he was able to accomplish what many have been trying to accomplish in their lifetime!

Jesus always said, "My Father said . . .; as my father does and whatever my father has shown me, that I do".

Could it be that the reason why many have failed the church and the society is because they are learning the wrong things because they have wrong teachers?

Who do you think the Holy Spirit is? Jesus handed over the work of growing the kingdom to his disciples and gave them the Holy Spirit. If you open your Bible, you will understand what Jesus was saying in John 14:26. He said that when the Holy Ghost shall come, he shall teach you ALL THINGS…

Why have we struggled so much with ignorance and lack of understanding? Because we neglect the Holy Spirit and are busy craving man's wisdom.

Don't get me wrong, I am not saying you should not learn from pastors or men of God; it is God who gave them abilities to gain the wisdom they teach. But, don't become dormant and dependent on another person's wisdom. Seek God and find the wealth of knowledge in him. No man can offer you what God can offer you, including wisdom and revelational knowledge.

In John 16:13, Jesus also referring to the Holy Spirit said "...he will guide you into ALL truth". The Spirit of God reveals things and also teaches. There is no kind of knowledge that you cannot access through the Holy Spirit.

Knowledge has increased on the earth, stop living like you are in the ages-past, find a relationship with the Holy Spirit and let him teach you. For sure, he will teach you well.

Additionally, whoever your teacher is, is who you will obey! This is just a reminder.

CONCLUSION

Satan Desires Worship

This is why it is said in the Bible how Lucifer, the son of the morning had fallen. Lucifer thought in his heart, "I will ascend above the heights...I will be like the Most-High " (Isaiah 14:14)KJV.

Here, being like the Most-High means to demand worship, and he is so thirsty for worship. He wants it from man. The man that was created in the very Image of God, that very image he wanted to be like. That is why Satan hates man so much, because he is jealous of man; you have what he desired from God, "being like the Most-High".

Lucifer was one of the most important angels that existed, and to raise another point, when anyone starts thinking that he or she is the most important person on earth, that individual needs to be careful; for sin is not far from that person. He was the anointed Cherub that Covered the Glory of God.

He saw the semblance of what being like God was. He was also a worship leader. Yes, Lucifer led worship from the earth to the heavens. He was the one that was given charge over Eden, the garden of God. Now, if you look at the book of Ezekiel 28:13, it says "Thou has been in Eden, the Garden of God..." KJV, and it talked about every precious stone that was his covering. This should tell you that when Lucifer was created, he was created on the earth and then placed in Eden just like man; to cover the glory of Eden. Let me clarify this saying; when Lucifer was created by God, He beautified him so much that his beauty became his pride. He was placed in Eden to keep charge over the Garden of God. In Eden the

Garden of God, the same Tree of the knowledge of good and evil, and the Tree of life was also in the middle of the garden, just as it was during the time of Adam. While he was to take charge of the Garden of God, he led worship to God. He was in charge of other created beings as man, which were called the stars of God. Man is the only being made in the image of God and this was after Lucifer rebelled against his maker.

While in this Garden of God, he began to traffic, experimenting with the fruits of the garden including the fruit from the Tree of the knowledge of good and evil. Additionally, he also ate the fruit from the Tree of Life, because he wanted to be like God. This is why he told the woman at the Garden and as captured in the book of Genesis 3:4-5 KJV "the serpent said unto the woman, Ye shall not surely die: For God doth know that in the day ye eat thereof, then your eyes shall be opened, and ye shall be as gods, knowing good and evil"! The serpent said you shall be as gods! Which gods was he talking about? He was talking about fallen angels who he corrupted with his traffic and convinced to eat of the same fruit.

This was also the main reason when Adam and the woman, ate the fruit, God had to send them away from the Garden saying "… Behold, the man is become as one of us, to know good and evil: and now, lest he put forth his hand, and take also of the tree of life, and eat, and live forever" Genesis 3:22 KJV. This should tell you that Lucifer ate the fruits from the Tree of knowledge of Good and Evil, and the Tree of Life; this is why he dwells perpetually as Satan and cannot be redeemed.

Furthermore, to avoid Adam and the woman Eve from being perpetually without redemption, God had to send them out of the Garden to prevent them from eating the Tree of Life and living for ever in that sinful nature. If Adam was to have eaten the fruit from the Tree of Life, he would have been irredeemable.

Now, if you study the devil very well, you will know that he has always used one tactics (deceit) against man; and that is all he is used to. That is all he knows, to try to convince people that what God said isn't true. He wants people to believe him, then get perverted in their thinking just like him.

In the process of leading worship, and having access to the holy mountain of God, sin perverted him when he desired to be like God. And because he had other angels lower than him, he also corrupted them with his perversion. That's what the Bible was talking about in the book of Ezekiel 28:16. It says "Through your widespread trade, you were filled with violence and you sinned. So, I drove you in disgrace from the mount of God, and I expelled you, guardian cherub, from among the fiery stones" NIV

Whenever the devil appears in any place or in anyone's life, his purpose is to take the place of God, to be worshiped, Satan desires that you worship him.

He entices people through their lustful desires and lures them to worship him using every means available. Whenever any individual has a series of challenges in any area, especially financially; it's Satan trying to stand in a place where he will force himself on that individual in order to extract worship.

When anyone falls victim of poverty, which is a form of bondage; it's because Satan is demanding worship; by oppressing that individual in that area. Have you noticed that for some people who worship the devil, he makes sure they have access to money. Whenever an individual is being lured into satanic worship, the first thing the devil promises that individual is the world in form of power and control. That is to make that individual famous; but how can one be famous without money? This is just a question; the devil gives access to wealth for control. Nonetheless, in return, the devil intends to control the life of that person, taking away control from that individual.

Many don't have control, because to have control, means to have money; money gives you a certain level of control over others. God has all the control, this is why the world is fighting so much to control how long people live on the earth, but it's never going to happen, because God has that control.

Anytime you encounter a situation that has refused to give in, look well, Satan is demanding your worship in that area.

This is why God said to Pharaoh to let my people go so they could worship me (Exodus 8:1). This is because you cannot worship God in truth and in spirit while in slavery or any form of bondage. Whoever is holding onto your miracle or breakthrough is the person that wants your worship. Whenever you believe man is the source of your breakthrough or miracles, you automatically switch whom you worship.

Satan is constantly trying to withstand the move of God or the authority of God for one reason. Just as a blasphemy unto God. To prove that he is also a god and also demanding to be worshiped. Any form of practice you perform, that's not in line to the worship of God, is a form of satanic worship.

Satan is not afraid of you

Satan is afraid of you knowing what he knows. Imagine what Jesus went through on the issue of his identity! Satan continued to say to him "If you are the son of God" (Luke 4-10).

Let me tell you something, Satan was an anointed Cherub, he was given power and he walked on the mountains of God. (Ezekiel 28:14-16). Read your Bible very well, he is not afraid of your anointing, he is only afraid of you knowing who you are. Once you know who you are, you can resist him, and he will flee. (James 4:7). The only way, you resist him is by submitting yourself to God.

Satan knows, once you know what he knows, then he is your footstool; he is under your foot. Why do you think Jesus said " Behold I have given you authority to step upon serpent (deceit) and upon scorpion, and ALL the power of the enemy... and nothing shall by ANY MEANS hurt you " (Luke 10:19) It is because Jesus understands your position on the earth. As a man created in the Image of God, you have authority over Satan. Look back to when God created man, He commanded man to have dominion over the work of His hands and over all the earth. (Genesis 1:26). This is the part of you that Satan hates the most; to know that you have dominion over him and over all of his work. He fights really hard to prevent you from understanding your authority over him. He will do anything to make sure you don't discover who you are in Christ. Additionally, more harm is to prevent you from believing in Jesus Christ. You can believe in any other god. This does not bother him, once you start heading towards Jesus, he trembles.

Satan's Ideology

Whenever Satan wants to deal with any individual (usually to kill, to steal and to destroy), he sells to that person an idea. This ideology is usually different from God's ideology.

The Woman (Eve) got an idea from the serpent that she was not like God, and she desired to be like God in her own lustfulness. She ate the fruit from the tree and lost what she was trying to be like; the image and the presence of God. Then, her eyes opened, and she saw that the covering she had which was the Glory of God, was just stolen. The serpent stripped her naked of the Glory, the very image of God.

The serpent tried so hard to convince the woman at the garden to see things from his own perspective. And as soon as she could see what he wanted her to see, she desired the fruit from the tree of the knowledge of good and evil. What the enemy is trying to show you is always contrary to what God is telling you. Guide your heart with all diligence...Proverb 4:23. Be wise! Whose ideology are you buying?

The anointing

An anointing gives you a level of independence from God. It's an ability to be a god and act like God. This is why God is very careful to give it out to people; because an anointing can destroy the carrier of it; if care is not taken.

An anointing brings you to the level of awareness with God, you possess power that God possess; and you can authoritatively order things to be, just like God. Anointing also opens your eyes to a different level of knowledge.

God has plenty of anointing, but very careful to give it out; because it intoxicates and if you don't have character, it will ruin you.

Lucifer was one of the cherubs in heaven, and God singled him out and gave him a little of himself, the anointing. You know, the anointing is part of what makes God who he is. Whenever God wants you to have a taste of who he is or what he looks like; He gives you a little of himself; the anointing.

As I was saying, Lucifer was favored out of other Cherubs and was given anointing for service. The Bible calls him an anointed cherub that covereth. He was fashioned differently with many instruments of music, along with precious stones. Additionally, he was assigned a position in the Garden of God. It is worthy to state that Lucifer was created on the earth with the same materials that could be found on the earth. How do I know this? Follow me to the book of Ezekiel 28:13. "Thou hast been in Eden the garden of God; every precious stone *was* thy covering, the sardius, topaz, and the diamond, the beryl, the onyx, and the jasper, the sapphire, the emerald, and the carbuncle, and gold: the workmanship of thy tabrets and of thy pipes was prepared in thee in the day that thou wast created" KJV.

These same precious stones were also in Eden when Adam was created. In the book of Genesis 2:10-12, it talked about the river that flowed out of Eden; the Garden that God planted and some of the contents of these rivers were the same precious material found in Lucifer. It means that Lucifer was created primarily to occupy Eden and was also given an ability to enter the mountain of God and walk in the midst of stones of fire, that is why he was freely moving in Eden when Adam and the Woman was there. He was able to manipulate the serpent to use him against the Woman. But you have to understand that it is for that very purpose that God gave Adam and the Woman dominion over everything on the earth, including the serpent. He was able to move freely on the space where God was, because he needed to account to God what was going on in his territory, the earth. It also means he was given so much to handle with so much liberty. His voice was like the sound of music, because of his very purpose, he was given an ability to function like God.

Since Lucifer lacked control, he began to traffic with merchandise that were meant to help him act like God. Perversion was into him because he developed some wrong thought process all together. His beauty and his level of independence corrupted him. Perversion was found in him.

This happens a lot when power is independent from the source. Your ability to act like God makes you vulnerable to sin.

If you understand this, then you can cling onto the one who gave you the power, to help provide checks and balances to you.

Men of God look at David, and they claim he was a murderer, yet God called him a man after my heart. The thing you don't understand is that there are different shades of God, if you hold onto his friendly shade for too long, you may become too familiar with him and forget that God is also known as a lawgiver, a judge (James 4:12) and an all-consuming fire.

The anointing gives you access to a certain information called classified information; some information that ordinarily you would never have if not for the anointing.

The information I share with you is because of the anointing which gave me access to some revelational knowledge of the Holy Spirit.

Don't get me wrong, every child of God has a level of the anointing released to them once they give their lives to Jesus. The Spirit of God comes on their inside to dwell. They can go further by allowing the anointing which is the person of the Holy Spirit to increase in measure. This is why Paul said, do not be drunk with wine, but be filled with the Holy Ghost. (5:18), which tells you that the anointing has measures.

As a Child of God, he will communicate to you not just his plans for you, but also the plans of the wicked one. Elisha would call up the King of Israel and give him classified information regarding the plans of the enemy for him. He would tell the king to avoid a certain route because his enemies were waiting for him there. (2Kings 6:8-12). These are the kind of information you would have as a child of God, depending on your level of yielding to the Holy Spirit. The deeper you go; the deeper the revelation you will have about God and the things that affect you and others.

Are you Hidden from the Devil?

If the devil spoke to Jesus, what makes you think you are safe from his voice?

Satan has been speaking and you cannot stop him from speaking. It's not time yet to silence him. At the final Judgment, he will be silenced.

Satan will continue to speak. He will speak to you in the form of terror and intimidation. If you permit, he will humiliate you. All that he says are lies, he was perverted from the very beginning and he will remain in his perversion, there is no redemption for Satan.

You are better off prepared to hear when he speaks and then respond to him the way Jesus responded to him. It's a big mistake to try to ignore the devil; ignoring him means you consent to whatever he is saying. This is why Paul said in Ephesians that after you have done all you need to do, stand your ground. (Ephesians 6:13)

Whenever the devil speaks, either through behaviors or voice, you stand your ground and place him where he belongs. If you think by ignoring that little witch or wizard in your family, it will make them to stop attacking you. You are very ignorant. They are supposed to stay away from you. They are supposed to know that you represent Jesus Christ in any environment you find yourself. This is what the enemy is afraid of.

Ignoring the devil is a big mistake. Don't ignore witchcraft, it's a bully and is the devil in manifestation. What do you do? Go deeper, seek God and as you seek, the Christ in you will begin to manifest physically. This is a problem for the kingdom of darkness. Have you ever read that you are the light of the world? Why are you trying to hide? That's the mistake you are making, you think if you hide, and stay away from them, they will leave you alone.

The more you try to hide, the more they take advantage of you. Stand up child of God, rule your territory, stand up for what is right, let the light of Christ in you shine through you. Let the light become heavy flames that it can burn off all the little devils around you.

This is what John was trying to say when he said that " the light shines in darkness and darkness comprehends it not" (John 1:5).

What am I trying to say? the more you try to hide, the more confused you become. Jesus was only a child, and in the stable, when his star was located. You can hide all you want; they will still locate you. Stop hiding, just stand your ground. When the devil finally speaks, as he is known as a speaking devil, be sure to place him where he belongs, under your feet. You can tell him it is written " ...we are seated in heavenly places in Christ Jesus " (Ephesians 2:6).

Inheriting the kingdom of God

The kingdom of God is a gift God gave to you in the person of Jesus Christ, but to inherit it is the gift; you will have to give to yourself.

In Luke 17:21, Jesus said that the kingdom of God is within you. And I am saying to you that even though the Kingdom of God is within you; because once you receive Jesus as your Lord and Savior, you entered the kingdom. Or better stated, the kingdom entered you. Nonetheless, you have work to do to actually inherit the kingdom of God.

Yes! Jesus paid the price by bringing the kingdom to you. However, you have work to do in order to inherit the kingdom. That is why Paul said in the book of Philippians 2:12 "work out your salvation with fear and trembling

The kingdom of God is not just God's system of governance, but also God's personality. The kingdom of God is not only a location; it is the person of Jesus Christ. This is why people enter in, but are not able to do exploit, because they never bothered to inherit the kingdom that they entered.

John the Baptist came with his gospel and he announced to the people to get ready, because the kingdom of God was at hand. (Mathew 3:2). He was pointing to the person of Jesus.

It is worthy to remember what Jesus said when he commissioned the Seventy. He said to tell people who were willing to receive their gospel that "...the kingdom of God is nigh unto you" (Luke 10:11) KJV. He further explained in Luke 17:20-21, when the Pharisees demanded to know when the Kingdom of God should be expected; saying to them they were making a mistake by trying to observe when the kingdom should come. He told them that the kingdom is already within them. Some other translations would say "among you" NIV

If Jesus said to the Pharisees that the kingdom was already among them, what Jesus was saying is for them to open their eyes to see that the one standing among them is the kingdom of God. He was literally telling them not to look any further because (HE) Jesus is the kingdom.

Paul said to the Corinthians when he was trying to address certain behaviors; that "the kingdom of God is not in words but in power "(1 Corinthians 4:20). If you are in the kingdom and cannot demonstrate power, you have not inherited the kingdom.

For more clarification, let's consider Apostle Paul's sayings in Galatians 5:19-21. He listed the things that cost many not to inherit the kingdom of God. "The acts of the flesh are obvious: sexual immorality, impurity and debauchery; idolatry and witchcraft; hatred, discord, jealousy, fits of rage, selfish ambition, dissensions, divisions and envy; drunkenness, orgies, and their like. I warn you, as I did before, that those who live like this will not inherit the kingdom of God" NIV

As long as you practice those things that Paul listed in Galatians 5:19-21, Paul says you cannot inherit the kingdom of God. You will be void of power and the manifestation of the characteristics of the Kingdom of God.

When you have inherited the kingdom of God, you are controlled by another realm and rules of that realm. You are then immune to the laws of nature, because the kingdom of God is not a place where nature rules. That is when you can walk on water, you can lay hands on the sick and diseases are healed. The devils will cry out for help when they see you, because the kingdom where you operate from, devils are not permitted.

Jesus said "I must also preach the kingdom of God to other cities also..." Luke 4:43. And when you read verses 40-42, you would understand what he referred to as preaching the Kingdom of God.

The gospel of Luke 4: 40-41NIV posits that:"At sunset, the people brought to Jesus all who had various kinds of sickness, and laying his hands on each one, he healed them. Moreover, demons came out of many people, shouting, "You are the Son of God!" But he rebuked them and would not allow them to speak, because they knew he was the Messiah"

Luke 4: 42 NKJ Now when it was day, He departed and went into a deserted place. And the crowd sought Him and came to Him and tried to keep Him from leaving them,

Luke 4: 43 (NKJV) but He said to them, "I must preach the kingdom of God to the other cities also, because for this purpose I have been sent."

Of a truth, any man of God who has not demonstrated Luke 4:40-41, has not quite inherited the Kingdom of God. Don't allow anyone to deceive you, the kingdom of God has been given to you, but you have to inherit this kingdom through faith and also by working out your salvation.

Jesus in one instance commanded the devil to come out of a person and he also command the devil to enter that person no more. Like in the case of the man whose son was possessed and tormented by the evil spirit, the one that the disciples couldn't cast out (Mark 9:17-27).

Both are authentic commands and the demon had to obey regardless if the house was well garnished or not. The command was to go and return no more. The demon aught not return to check if the house is still available or not. The order is an order and it's authentic.

It is just like a restraining order, when you are told not to be found within certain miles around a person, you can't do otherwise. If you dare, there will be consequences. Demons know their limits. Just like Satan their master. "You go and return no more", that's a spiritual order and must be obeyed!

If those demons had tried to defy that order, it would have resulted in dangerous consequences. There are unseen angels who wait to make sure an order is obeyed. They enforce these orders.

Christianity is not void of power, the kingdom of God that we preach is not void of power. It is the people that are void of power, because they have allowed the world to enter into the church. Additionally, corruption has turned the church into a marketplace. Jesus said, "My house shall be called a house of prayer..." (Mathew 21:13)KJV.

Satan is walking around, negotiating the kingdom of God with people of God. He is a trafficker and that is what he knows how to do best.

This is why, a man or woman of God can just finish sinning and go back to hold the microphone and lay filthy hands on the people of God. At the end, no healing and no manifestation of the Kingdom because they don't have it. A popular legal statement written in Latin "Nemo dat quod non habet" meaning you can't give what you don't have. Many are trying to give the people of God the kingdom that they have not inherited; though they are in the kingdom, they have not inherited the kingdom, and are unable to give it out.

This is why I say to you like Paul the apostle, the kingdom of God is not in words or display of ignorance, let it be about the manifestation of the power of God. For where the word of a king is, there is power (Eccl 8:4).

Finally, I am not ignorant of this glaring fact, that the devil is so desperate to have the people of God; to have me. He is so proud and cannot imagine submitting to man after walking up and down the mountain of the Lord. He finds it difficult to imagine. The devil is afraid of you thinking on your own; he wants to think for you, it's called deceit.

How do you tell a woman that was created in the image of God that she would be like God if she eats a fruit? The one being spoken to, didn't use her thinking ability to question the serpent? If I am already like Him (God) because I was made in his image, why do I need to be like Him again? But the woman like I said wasn't thinking? The serpent actually told her she would be like the "gods" KJV. Which means the serpent knew what he was doing and saying, only the woman didn't know what she was doing and being told. You will be like the "gods" (idols). The Hebrew word used there "gods" is "ke-lo-him" the same word used for "sons of god, or angels" the same word could also be used for gods and goddess. Why would you go from being like God to being like angels? Going from an image of authority and power to a lesser image?

This is the same thing he is still doing today, the same story from the beginning; switching places with man.

Only the devil knows when he is deceiving you, the deceived usually has no clue because he is so enticed in his lust! Open your eyes whenever you are being offered something, if you have a question? Then you should really think about it.

All Satan wants to do is to stop you from getting to the Source, because what the Source has in stuck for you is overwhelmingly great. This is why he wants to negotiate with you over your worship.

Jesus Christ is so jealous over his church, he gave us guaranteed coverage, the Holy Spirit.

Satan has desperately desired me, he wants me dead or alive, but he cannot have me either way.

I know for a fact that there is a price tag on me by the devil, but he couldn't have me, even though he doesn't really give up. I am taken; I belong to Jesus Christ!

SHALOM!

ABOUT THE AUTHOR

Dr Chioma Afoke is An STD (Sexually Transmitted Disease) Prevention Scholar, with A Doctorate Degree In Nursing Practice. She is a Graduate of Rutgers State University of New Jersey. A Certified Family Nurse Practitioner with publications from the Center for disease Prevention and Control (CDC). She is also a member of the American Public Health Association (APHA).

Dr Afoke is married to Christian Afoke PhD, and they both have three beautiful children, Jedidiah, Zephaniah, and Serach Afoke.

With an exceptional revelational knowledge of the word of God inspired by the Holy Spirit, Chioma has decided to begin to share her knowledge of the kingdom of God, with the world. Knowing that, these things being constantly revealed to her are not just for her own consumptions, the world is in need of more Knowledge of who God is, and what the church represents to the world. We, the church as the body of Christ, are the carriers of the Kingdom of God!

Printed in the United States
By Bookmasters